Smoking Bans
Second Edition

POINT
COUNTERPOINT

Smoking Bans
Second Edition

David L. Hudson Jr.

Series Consulting Editor
Alan Marzilli, M.A., J.D.

CHELSEA HOUSE
PUBLISHERS
An imprint of Infobase Publishing

Library of Congress Cataloging-in-Publication Data

Hudson, David L., 1969–
    Smoking bans / by David L. Hudson. — 2nd ed.
       p. cm. — (Point/counterpoint)
    Includes bibliographical references and index.
    ISBN 978-0-7910-9795-3 (hardcover : acid-free paper) 1. Smoking—United
States—Juvenile literature. 2. Smoking—Law and legislation—United States—
Juvenile literature. 3. Tobacco industry—United States—Juvenile literature.
I. Title. II. Series.

    HV5760.H83 2008
    362.29'60973—dc22   2008014624

Alan Marzilli, M.A., J.D.
Washington, D.C.

The POINT/COUNTERPOINT series offers the reader a greater under-standing of some of the most controversial issues in contemporary American society—issues such as capital punishment, immigration, gay rights, and gun control. We have looked for the most contem-porary issues and have included topics—such as the controversies surrounding "blogging"—that we could not have imagined when the series began.

In each volume, the author has selected an issue of particular importance and set out some of the key arguments on both sides of the issue. Why study both sides of the debate? Maybe you have yet to make up your mind on an issue, and the arguments presented in the book will help you to form an opinion. More likely, however, you will already have an opinion on many of the issues covered by the series. There is always the chance that you will change your opinion after reading the arguments for the other side. But even if you are firmly committed to an issue—for example, school prayer or animal rights—reading both sides of the argument will help you to become a more effective advo-cate for your cause. By gaining an understanding of opposing argu-ments, you can develop answers to those arguments.

Perhaps more importantly, listening to the other side sometimes helps you see your opponent's arguments in a more human way. For example, Sister Helen Prejean, one of the nation's most visible oppo-nents of capital punishment, has been deeply affected by her interac-tions with the families of murder victims. By seeing the families' grief and pain, she understands much better why people support the death penalty, and she is able to carry out her advocacy with a greater sensi-tivity to the needs and beliefs of death penalty supporters.

The books in the series include numerous features that help the reader to gain a greater understanding of the issues. Real-life examples illustrate the human side of the issues. Each chapter also includes excerpts from relevant laws, court cases, and other material, which provide a better foundation for understanding the arguments. The volumes contain citations to relevant sources of law and information, and an appendix guides the reader through the basics of legal research, both on the Internet and in the library. Today, through free Web sites, it is easy to access legal documents, and these books might give you ideas for your own research.

Studying the issues covered by the Point-Counterpoint series is more than an academic activity. The issues described in the book affect all of us as citizens. They are the issues that today's leaders debate and tomorrow's leaders will decide. While all of the issues covered in the Point-Counterpoint series are controversial today, and will remain so for the foreseeable future, it is entirely possible that the reader might one day play a central role in resolving the debate. Today it might seem that some debates—such as capital punishment and abortion—will never be resolved.

However, our nation's history is full of debates that seemed as though they never would be resolved, and many of the issues are now well settled—at least on the surface. In the nineteenth century, abolitionists met with widespread resistance to their efforts to end slavery. Ultimately, the controversy threatened the union, leading to the Civil War between the northern and southern states. Today, while a public debate over the merits of slavery would be unthinkable, racism persists in many aspects of society.

Similarly, today nobody questions women's right to vote. Yet at the beginning of the twentieth century, suffragists fought public battles for women's voting rights, and it was not until the passage of the Nineteenth Amendment in 1920 that the legal right of women to vote was established nationwide.

What makes an issue controversial? Often, controversies arise when most people agree that there is a problem, but people disagree about the best way to solve the problem. There is little argument that poverty is a major problem in the United States, especially in inner cities and rural areas. Yet, people disagree vehemently about the best way to address the problem. To some, the answer is social programs, such as welfare, food stamps, and public housing. However, many argue that such subsidies encourage dependence on government benefits while unfairly penalizing those who work and pay taxes, and that the real solution is to require people to support themselves.

American society is in a constant state of change, and sometimes modern practices clash with what many consider to be "traditional values," which are often rooted in conservative political views or religious beliefs. Many blame high crime rates, and problems such as poverty, illiteracy, and drug use on the breakdown of the traditional family structure of a married mother and father raising their children. Since the "sexual revolution" of the 1960s and 1970s, sparked in part by the widespread availability of the birth control pill, marriage rates have declined, and the number of children born outside of marriage has increased. The sexual revolution led to controversies over birth control, sex education, and other issues, most prominently abortion. Similarly, the gay rights movement has been challenged as a threat to traditional values. While many gay men and lesbians want to have the same right to marry and raise families as heterosexuals, many politicians and others have challenged gay marriage and adoption as a threat to American society.

Sometimes, new technology raises issues that we have never faced before, and society disagrees about the best solution. Are people free to swap music online, or does this violate the copyright laws that protect songwriters and musicians' ownership of the music that they create? Should scientists use "genetic engineering" to create new crops that are resistant to disease and pests and produce more food, or is it too risky to use a laboratory to create plants that nature never intended? Modern medicine has continued to increase the average lifespan—which is now 77 years, up from under 50 years at the beginning of the twentieth century—but many people are now choosing to die in comfort rather than living with painful ailments in their later years. For doctors, this presents an ethical dilemma: should they allow their patients to die? Should they assist patients in ending their own lives painlessly?

Perhaps the most controversial issues are those that implicate a Constitutional right. The Bill of Rights—the first 10 Amendments to the U.S. Constitution—spell out some of the most fundamental rights that distinguish our democracy from other nations with fewer freedoms. However, the sparsely-worded document is open to interpretation, with each side saying that the Constitution is on their side. The Bill of Rights was meant to protect individual liberties; however, the needs of some individuals clash with society's needs. Thus, the Constitution often serves as a battleground between individuals and government officials seeking to protect society in some way. The First Amendment's guarantee of "freedom of speech" leads to some very difficult questions. Some forms of expression—such as burning an American flag—lead to public outrage, but are protected by the First Amendment. Other types of expression that most people find objectionable—such as child pornography—are not protected by the Constitution. The question is not only where to draw the line, but whether drawing lines around constitutional rights threatens our liberty.

The Bill of Rights raises many other questions about individual rights and societal "good." Is a prayer before a high school football game an "establishment of religion" prohibited by the First Amendment? Does the Second Amendment's promise of "the right to bear arms" include concealed handguns? Does stopping and frisking someone standing on a known drug corner constitute "unreasonable search and seizure" in violation of the Fourth Amendment? Although the U.S. Supreme Court has the ultimate authority in interpreting the U.S. Constitution, their answers do not always satisfy the public. When a group of nine people—sometimes by a five-to-four vote—makes a decision that affects hundreds of millions of others, public outcry can be expected. For example, the Supreme Court's 1973 ruling in Roe v. Wade that abortion is protected by the Constitution did little to quell the debate over abortion.

Whatever the root of the controversy, the books in the Point-Counterpoint series seek to explain to the reader both the origins of the debate, the current state of the law, and the arguments on either side of the debate. Our hope in creating this series is that the reader will be better informed about the issues facing not only our politicians, but all of our nation's citizens, and become more actively involved in resolving these debates, as voters, concerned citizens, journalists, or maybe even elected officials.

The History of Tobacco and Its Regulation

Tobacco has been a staple in American society since its introduction more than 400 years ago. It became a leading crop for many early American colonies and continued to drive the economy of those colonies as they entered statehood. Even today, it remains a major force as American tobacco companies gross billions of dollars each year. Millions of Americans and people worldwide regularly use cigarettes, cigars, and other tobacco products. However, tobacco also has long been a burning controversy in society. It is, in the words of the U.S. Department of Justice, "the single leading cause of preventable death in the United States."[1]

People have railed against tobacco for hundreds of years. As early as 1604, Britain's King James I attacked tobacco in his treatise *A Counter-Blaste to Tobacco*. He described tobacco smoking as "a custom loathsome to the eye, hateful to the nose, harmful to the brain, dangerous to the lung, and the black stinking fume thereof, nearest resembling the horribly Stygian smoke of the pit that is bottomless."[2]

By the end of the seventeenth century, leading practitioners of medicine in Paris began to suspect that tobacco was harmful to humans. In 1853, physician L.B. Coles called tobacco "a deadly narcotic" in his book *The Beauties and Deformities of Tobacco-Using*.[3] Such views were in the minority, though. Most of those opposed to tobacco criticized smoking on moral grounds, not for the health reasons cited in today's debates. Furthermore, most members of the medical community and the

Smoking and Religion

Although some traditional religions have been known to use smoking as part of ritual, no modern religion actively encourages the use of tobacco by members. In fact, many faiths forbid tobacco entirely.

During the month of fasting of Ramadan, Muslims are required to give up smoking—including passive, or secondhand, smoking.

Several branches of Christianity forbid smoking by adherents, including:

American Society of Friends (Quakers)
Methodist Church
Baptists
Mormons (Church of Jesus Christ of Latter-day Saints)
The Salvation Army
Seventh-Day Adventists

Hinduism, too, discourages smoking. According to Hindu religious leader Swami Amarananda of the Hindu Centre of Geneva, "Tobacco is traditionally seen as a *vyasana* or an unhealthy dependence. And the goal of spiritual life lies in the cessation of suffering, access to bliss and freedom from the bondage of nature. So a *vyasana* matches ill with a spiritual life."*

*Quoted in Subhamoy Das, "Unholy Smoke!" Available online. URL: http://hinduism.about. com/library/weekly/aa052900a.htm.

general public viewed smoking as something that could be done in moderation.

At the end of the nineteenth century, only one in a hundred Americans smoked tobacco. Around that time, several states including Iowa, Tennessee, and North Dakota outlawed the sale of cigarettes. A suit was filed concerning the Tennessee law, which outlawed the selling or giving away of "cigarettes, cigarette paper, or substitute for the same." The penalty for breaking this law was a $50 fine. In 1900, the U.S. Supreme Court ruled in *Austin v. Tennessee* that the state could lawfully ban the product because of its (the state's) general power to protect public heath and welfare.[4]

Even though the Court would not demonize tobacco as an inherently harmful product, it recognized that the Tennessee law was "designed for the protection of the public health."[5] The defendant, William B. Austin, had purchased large quantities of cigarettes from the American Tobacco Company in Durham, North Carolina, and then sold them in Tennessee. He argued that the state law violated the commerce clause of the U.S. Constitution. The commerce clause provides that Congress—and only Congress—has the power to regulate commerce between the states, called interstate commerce. Tennessee countered that it had the right under its general police power to protect the health of its citizenry. In siding with Tennessee, the U.S. Supreme Court wrote that the state could not "force into the markets of a state, against its will, articles or commodities which, like cigarettes, may not unreasonably be held to be injurious to health."[6]

In 1920, the Eighteenth Amendment went into effect, providing for the start of Prohibition. The amendment prohibited the sale and distribution of alcohol. Tobacco industry executives feared their product would be next. Government officials did not ban cigarettes, however. Instead, they taxed them. In 1921, Iowa became the first state to tax cigarettes.[7]

Tobacco has a long history in the United States, stretching back to its beginnings as a cash crop in the first American colonies. Here, a farm worker in Georgia lifts a tray of young tobacco plants at the beginning of the planting season in 2004.

Although efforts were made to enforce the ban on alcoholic beverages, many people found ways to illegally buy and sell liquor. It eventually became clear that Prohibition was not working. The Eighteenth Amendment was repealed with the Twenty-first Amendment, which took effect in 1933. The era of Prohibition was over.

In the twentieth century, the medical community began to realize more and more the dangers of smoking. In 1939, Franz Hermann Muller of the University of Cologne's Pathological

FROM THE BENCH

Austin v. Tennessee, 179 U.S. 343 (1900)

Cigarettes do not seem until recently to have attracted the attention of the public as more injurious than other forms of tobacco; nor are we now prepared to take judicial notice of any special injury resulting from their use or to indorse the opinion of the supreme court of Tennessee that "they are inherently bad and bad only."...Without undertaking to affirm or deny their evil effects, we think it within the province of the legislature to say how far they may be sold, or to prohibit their sale entirely, after they have been taken from the original packages or have left the hands of the importer, provided no discrimination be used as against such as are imported from other states, and there be no reason to doubt that the act in question is designed for the protection of the public health.

We have had repeated occasion to hold, where state legislation has been attacked as violative either of the power of Congress over interstate commerce, or of the 14th Amendment to the Constitution, that, if the action of the state legislature were as a bona fide exercise of its police power, and dictated by a genuine regard for the preservation of the public health or safety, such legislation would be respected, though it might interfere indirectly with interstate commerce....

We are therefore of opinion that although the state of Tennessee may not wholly interdict commerce in cigarettes it is not, in the language of Chief Justice Taney in *The License Cases*, "bound to furnish a market for it [them], nor to abstain from the passage of any law which it may deem necessary or advisable to guard the health or morals of its citizens, although such law may discourage importation, or diminish the profits of the importer, or lessen the revenue of the general government."...

Most pertinent to this case, and, as we think, covering its principle completely, is the opinion of this court in *May v. New Orleans*, 178 U.S. 496, 44 L. ed. 1165, 20 Sup. Ct. Rep. 976....This involved the validity of certain tax assessments made by the city of New Orleans upon the merchandise and stock in trade of the plaintiff, which consisted of dry goods imported from foreign countries, upon which duties had been levied by and paid to the general government. The goods were put up and sold in packages, a large number of such packages being inclosed in wooden cases or boxes for the purposes of importation. Upon arrival at New Orleans the boxes were opened, the packages taken out and sold unbroken. The question was whether the box or case containing these packages, or the packages themselves were the original packages within the case of *Brown v. Maryland*, 12 Wheat. 419, 6 L. ed. 678. It was conceded that, so long as the packages remained in their original cases, they were not subject to taxation, but the court held that this immunity ceased as soon as the boxes were opened....

The real question in this case is whether the size of the package in which the importation is actually made is to govern; or, the size of the package in which bona fide transactions are carried on between the manufacturer and the whole-sale dealer residing in different states. We hold to the latter view. The whole theory of the exemption of the original package from the operation of state laws is based upon the idea that the property is imported in the ordinary form in which, from time immemorial, foreign goods have been brought into the country. These have gone at once into the hands of the wholesale dealers, who have been in the habit of breaking the packages and distributing their contents among the several retail dealers throughout the state. It was with reference to this method of doing business that the doctrine of the exemption of the original package grew up. But taking the words "original package" in their literal sense, a number of so-called original package manufactories have been started through the country, whose business it is to manufacture goods for the express purpose of sending their products into other states in minute packages, that may at once go into the hands of the retail dealers and consumers, and thus bid defiance to the laws of the state against their importation and sale.... This court has repeatedly held that, so far from lending its authority to frauds upon the sanitary laws of the several states, we are bound to respect such laws and to aid in their enforcement, so far as can be done without infringing upon the constitutional rights of the parties. The consequences of our adoption of defendant's contention would be far reaching and disastrous....

The question is not in what packages the law requires the cigarettes to be packed for the purpose of taxation, but, what are the packages in which they are usually transported from one state to another where the transaction is bona fide and for the legitimate purposes of trade and commerce?

We are satisfied the conclusion of the Supreme Court of Tennessee was correct, and it is therefore affirmed.

Institute in Germany observed that the increase in smoking after World War I "runs parallel with the increase in primary lung cancer."[8]

Despite such findings, however, tobacco became immensely popular. World War II led to a further increase in smoking. By 1950, 50 percent of American adults smoked tobacco.[9] Author and journalist Richard Kluger writes, "the cultural habituation of Americans to their cigarettes was seductively advanced by Hollywood."[10]

In the 1940s and 1950s, the Federal Trade Commission (FTC) began to police the tobacco companies for their advertisements that cigarettes were harmless. By the end of 1953, the American Medical Association (AMA) stopped accepting cigarette ads in its leading scientific journal, *Journal of the American Medical Association*. That same year, Dr. Ernst Wynder published a study in the magazine *Cancer Research* examining the effects of tobacco exposure on mice. He painted a group of mice with tobacco smoke. Twenty months later, only 10 percent of the painted animals were still alive, while 58 percent of the unpainted mice had survived. "On many fronts and in many laboratories, the case against smoking grew in the late fifties," writes Kluger.[11]

The tobacco companies were worried about these medical studies. They enlisted the services of a leading public relations firm and formed the Tobacco Industry Research Committee. The tobacco companies engaged in a concentrated process of research and public relations. Still, for every dollar spent on research, tobacco companies spent $200 on the advertisement and promotion of their products.[12]

The tobacco companies managed to convince many members of the public that smoking really wasn't that bad. In 1964, a leading tobacco executive told the *New York Times*, "I don't believe the present product will prove to be a health hazard." At the same time, a few people involved in research for the tobacco companies recognized the dangers. A 1961 memo drafted by a scientist for Philip Morris stated, "A morally acceptable low-carcinogen cigarette may be possible. Its development will require TIME, MONEY and UNFAILING DETERMINATION."[13]

The Surgeon General's Advisory Committee on Smoking and Health conducted its first meeting in November 1962. The committee issued a 387-page report concluding, "Cigarette smoking is a health hazard of sufficient importance in the United States to warrant appropriate remedial action."[14] The public soon began to realize the harms of smoking, too. A 1968 Gallup poll reported that 71 percent of the public believed that smoking caused cancer. Just 10 years before, only 44 percent had believed that.

Still, tobacco use continued. Wrote Kluger: "As the scientific evidence against it gathered throughout the 1950s, the tobacco industry did not merely deny, dispute, and mock it as a defensive strategy; it also spent heavily on advertising as its prime offensive weapon to convince its customers that the product was well worth any risk that might accompany their use of it."[15]

Gradually, a consensus grew within the medical and scientific community that smoking had harmful effects upon public health. This led to increased calls for bans on smoking in public places. Many states began to pass so-called clean indoor air acts. To this day, litigation continues as more and more states and municipalities impose smoking bans, even in places traditionally associated with smoking, such as bars.

The public health findings on smoking have also led to increasing numbers of lawsuits against the tobacco industry. First individuals, then classes of individuals, and even state attorneys general began to file suit against tobacco companies. They accused companies of fraud and deceit in marketing an addictive product while concealing just how addictive and harmful their products are.

Smoking remains a controversial issue. "No one could seriously dispute that today smoking is a social and political issue of enormous intensity and import," writes law professor Martin Redish. "The smoking controversy involves a variety of heavily

FROM THE BENCH

FDA v. Brown & Williamson Tobacco Corporation, 592 U.S. 120 (2000)

In 1996, the Food and Drug Administration (FDA), after having expressly disavowed any such authority since its inception, asserted jurisdiction to regulate tobacco products.... The FDA concluded that nicotine is a "drug" within the meaning of the Food, Drug, and Cosmetic Act (FDCA or Act) ... and that cigarettes and smokeless tobacco are "combination products" that deliver nicotine to the body.... Pursuant to this authority, it promulgated regulations intended to reduce tobacco consumption among children and adolescents.... The agency believed that, because most tobacco consumers begin their use before reaching the age of 18, curbing tobacco use by minors could substantially reduce the prevalence of addiction in future generations and thus the incidence of tobacco-related death and disease....

Regardless of how serious the problem an administrative agency seeks to address, however, it may not exercise its authority "in a manner that is inconsistent with the administrative structure that Congress enacted into law." ... In this case, we believe that Congress has clearly precluded the FDA from asserting jurisdiction to regulate tobacco products. In light of this clear intent, the FDA's assertion of jurisdiction is impermissible....

The FDA promulgated these regulations pursuant to its authority to regulate "restricted devices" ... using the Act's drug authorities, device authorities, or both, depending on "how the public health goals of the act can be best accomplished." ... Given the greater flexibility in the FDCA for the regulation of devices, the FDA determined that "the device authorities provide the most appropriate basis for regulating cigarettes and smokeless tobacco." ... Under 21 U.S.C. 360j(e), the agency may "require that a device be restricted to sale, distribution, or use ... upon such other conditions as [the FDA] may prescribe in such regulation, if, because of its potentiality for harmful effect or the collateral measures necessary to its use, [the FDA] determines that there cannot otherwise be reasonable assurance of its safety and effectiveness."

Respondents, a group of tobacco manufacturers, retailers, and advertisers, filed suit in United States District Court for the Middle District of North Carolina challenging the regulations.... They moved for summary judgment on the grounds that the FDA lacked jurisdiction to regulate tobacco products as customarily marketed, the regulations exceeded the FDA's authority under 21 U.S.C. 360j(e), and the advertising restrictions violated the First Amendment.... The court held that the FDCA authorizes the FDA to regulate tobacco products as customarily marketed and that the FDA's access and labeling regulations are permissible, but it also found that the agency's advertising and promotion restrictions exceed its authority under §360j(e).... The court stayed implementation of the regulations it found valid (except the prohibition on the sale of tobacco products to minors) and certified its order for immediate interlocutory appeal....

The Court of Appeals for the Fourth Circuit reversed, holding that Congress has not granted the FDA jurisdiction to regulate tobacco products.... Examining the FDCA as a whole, the court concluded that the FDA's regulation of tobacco products would create a number of internal inconsistencies.... Various provisions of the Act require the agency to determine that any regulated product is "safe" before it can be sold or allowed to remain on the market, yet the FDA found in its rule-making proceeding that tobacco products are "dangerous"and "unsafe." Thus, the FDA would apparently have to ban tobacco products, a result the court found clearly contrary to congressional intent. This apparent anomaly, the Court of Appeals concluded, demonstrates that Congress did not intend to give the FDA authority to regulate tobacco. The court also found that evidence external to the FDCA confirms this conclusion. Importantly, the FDA consistently stated before 1995 that it lacked jurisdiction over tobacco, and Congress has enacted several tobacco-specific statutes fully cognizant of the FDA's position. In fact, the court reasoned, Congress has considered and rejected many bills that would have given the agency such authority. This, along with the absence of any intent by the enacting Congress in 1938 to subject tobacco products to regulation under the FDCA, demonstrates that Congress intended to withhold such authority from the FDA.

A threshold issue is the appropriate framework for analyzing the FDA's assertion of authority to regulate tobacco products. Because this case involves an administrative agency's construction of a statute that it administers...a reviewing court must first ask "whether Congress has directly spoken to the precise question at issue." If Congress has done so, the inquiry is at an end; the court "must give effect to the unambiguously expressed intent of Congress."...

With these principles in mind, we find that Congress has directly spoken to the issue here and precluded the FDA's jurisdiction to regulate tobacco products.

...[I]t is clear that Congress intended to exclude tobacco products from the FDA's jurisdiction.

contested issues, implicating questions of scientific theory, individual free choice, social responsibility, and the scope of governmental power."[16] Looming questions remain regarding the constitutionality of smoking bans, product liability suits against tobacco companies, and restriction of tobacco advertising. Another contested issue concerns the large donations made to political candidates by the tobacco industry. Antismoking advocates recently released a study showing that tobacco interests spent more than $20 million in 2002 to lobby political leaders.[17]

Still another major issue concerns the Food and Drug Administration (FDA) and its failed attempts to regulate tobacco. In 2000, the U.S. Supreme Court ruled in *FDA v. Brown & Williamson Tobacco Corp.* that the FDA did not have the authority to regulate tobacco as a drug.[18] However, measures have since been introduced in Congress to give the FDA the necessary authority to regulate tobacco.

This book examines three major controversies that involve smoking, including: (1) smoking bans; (2) tort lawsuits filed against tobacco companies for injuries suffered by smokers and those harmed by secondhand smoke; and (3) restrictions on tobacco advertising.

Smoking Bans Protect Public Health

Gail Routh worked as a flight attendant for 27 years, beginning in 1972. A nonsmoker all her life, Routh nonetheless contracted lung cancer after working in close contact with secondhand smoke on airplanes in the years before smoking was banned on airline flights. Routh sued Philip Morris U.S.A., R.J. Reynolds Tobacco Co., Lorillard Tobacco, and Brown & Williamson Tobacco Corporation, claiming that the exposure to secondhand smoke had caused both her lung cancer and conditions of chronic sinusitis and bronchitis.

But in October 2003, a Florida jury decided against Routh. Although the jury declared that secondhand smoke could be a cause of cancer, it could not be proven conclusively that it had been the cause of Routh's own medical conditions. The verdict surprised many observers. "This is a woman who was healthy as could be when she started working in 1972, a lifetime non-smoker who had no medical problems," argued the lawyer who represented Routh in the case. "Everything points to secondhand smoke as the cause."[1]

Smokers often insist they have the individual right to smoke. Smoking, after all, is still a legal activity for adults. But non-smokers have rights, too. The personal preferences of smokers should not trump the right of nonsmokers to breathe clean air in a healthy environment. In other words, smokers may have the right to harm their own health but not the health of others.

The clear trend in American society is to segregate, if not eliminate, smoking in public places. Smoking is prohibited in airplanes, sports stadiums, places of employment, and many restaurants. Nonsmokers have successfully petitioned city and state legislators for an increasing array of smoking restrictions. Many state and local governments have responded with broad

THE LETTER OF THE LAW

Calabasas, California, Anti-Secondhand Smoke Ordinance

(a) No person, Employer, Business, or Nonprofit Entity shall knowingly permit Smoking in an area under his, her, or its legal or de facto control in which smoking is prohibited by this chapter or other law.

(b) No person, Employer, Business, or Nonprofit Entity shall allow the placement or maintenance of a receptacle for Smoking waste in an area under his, her, or its legal or de facto control in which smoking is prohibited by this chapter or other law.

(c) Notwithstanding any other provision of this chapter, any owner, landlord, Employer, Business, Nonprofit Entity, or other person who or which has legal or de facto control over any property may declare any area in which Smoking would otherwise be permitted to be a nonsmoking area and, provided that signs are posted giving notice of the Smoking restriction, Smoking in or within a Reasonable Distance of that area shall constitute a violation of this chapter.

restrictions on smokers. The state of Delaware passed a law prohibiting smoking in "any indoor enclosed area to which the general public is invited or in which the general public is permitted."[2] New York City (2002) and Dallas (2003) are two examples of cities that have recently passed highly restrictive smoking laws. Commentators estimated in a 2002 article that more than 1,400 local jurisdictions across the United States have passed antismoking regulations.[3]

In Calabasas, California, legislators passed a law banning smoking in any public place where others could smell cigarette smoke. In the summer of 2007, legislators thought of extending the ban to make apartments smoke-free, prohibiting smokers from puffing in their own apartments.[4]

Scientific evidence confirms that smoking—including inhaling secondhand smoke—is harmful. The Environmental Protection Agency (EPA) estimates that there are at least 3,000 lung

(d) "No Smoking" or "Smoke Free" signs, with letters of no less than one inch in height or the international "No Smoking" symbol (consisting of a pictorial representation of a burning cigarette enclosed in a red circle with a red bar across it) or any alternative signage approved by the community development director of the city shall be conspicuously posted at each entrance to a Public Place in which Smoking is prohibited by this chapter, by the person, Employer, Business, or Nonprofit Entity who or which has legal or de facto control of such place. The city manager shall post signs at each entrance to a Public Place in which Smoking is prohibited by this Chapter which is owned or controlled by the city. Signage required by this paragraph shall not be subject to chapter 17.30 ("Signs") of this code. Notwithstanding this provision, the presence or absence of signs shall not be a defense to the violation of any other provision of this chapter except as to an area in which Smoking is prohibited only by paragraph (c) of this subsection.

Source: Calabasas Ordinance Against Secondhand Smoke. Available online. URL: http://www.cityofcalabasas.com/pdf/agendas/council/2006/021506/item2-O2006-217.pdf.

cancer deaths each year from secondhand smoke.[5] In addition to that, secondhand smoke causes 46,000 cardiac deaths in the United States annually.[6] One study in England showed that asthmatic children exposed to secondhand smoke spend more time in hospitals and recover less quickly.[7] And Tennessee governor Phil Bredesen has said that smoking adds $2 billion in annual health care costs to his state alone.[8]

In 1964, the U.S. Surgeon General declared that smoking was a health hazard and causally related to lung cancer. The next year, the U.S. Congress passed the Cigarette Labeling and Advertising Act, which required cigarette manufacturers to include warning labels on all cigarette advertisements. The mandated warning read: "Caution: cigarette smoking may be hazardous to your health."[9] In 1970, Congress amended the law in the Public Health Cigarette Smoking Act to require an even stricter message: "Warning: The Surgeon General Has Determined That Cigarette Smoking Is Dangerous To Your Health."[10]

In 1986, the U.S. Surgeon General declared that even inhaling another person's cigarette smoke was harmful. Environmental tobacco smoke (ETS), also called secondhand smoke, consists of sidestream smoke and mainstream smoke. Sidestream smoke is the smoke emitted from the tip of a burning cigarette. Mainstream smoke is the smoke exhaled by the smoker.

In 1993, a report by the Environmental Protection Agency concluded: "Based on the weight of the available scientific evidence, the U.S. Environmental Protection Agency (EPA) has concluded that the widespread exposure to ETS in the United States presents a serious and substantial public health impact."[11] The report added that for adults, "ETS is a human lung carcinogen, responsible for approximately 3,000 lung cancer deaths annually in U.S. nonsmokers."[12] The National Cancer Institute reported that there are many harmful effects associated with ETS, including: "disease and premature death in nonsmoking adults and children. . . . It may increase the risk of heart disease by an estimated 25 to 30 percent. . . . Children exposed to secondhand smoke are at an increased risk of sudden infant death syndrome (SIDS), ear infections, colds, pneumonia, bronchitis, and more severe asthma."[13]

In sum, there is no doubt that smoking affects more than just the health of smokers. Nonsmokers who are exposed to smoking can also suffer harm. For this reason alone, smoking bans serve the public interest in the health, safety, and welfare of nonsmokers and children.

Smoking bans in the workplace are justified.

Smoking bans in the workplace are essential for the health and well-being of employees. Employers have a common law duty to provide a safe and healthy working environment for employees. In 1976, a New Jersey court determined that an employer had a duty to shield its employees from the noxious effects of smoking. The case arose after Donna Shimp sued her employer, New Jersey Bell Telephone Company, for failing to protect her from cigarette smoke.

Shimp alleged that cigarette smoke at work caused her to suffer severe throat irritation, nasal irritation, eye irritation, headaches, nausea, and vomiting. The Superior Court of New Jersey determined that the telephone company must enforce a no-smoking policy. It declared: "There can be no doubt that the by-products of burning tobacco are toxic and dangerous to the health of smokers and nonsmokers generally and this plaintiff in particular."[14] In making its findings, the court cited evidence from the U.S. Surgeon General, as well as experts in cardiovascular disease, allergy and immunology, and occupational safety. "The employees' right to a safe working environment makes it clear that smoking must be forbidden in the work area," the court wrote.[15]

Other courts have determined that employees can sue to force their employers to prohibit or limit smoking in the workplace. In 2003, a federal appeals court reinstated a suit brought by a federal railroad worker who alleged that his severe asthma was

Smoking bans in the workplace

A total of 16 states and the District of Columbia have banned smoking in private workplaces, which do not include restaurants and bars. Similar bans exist on the local level in other states also.

Percentage of population covered by state or local laws that ban smoking in public and private workplaces

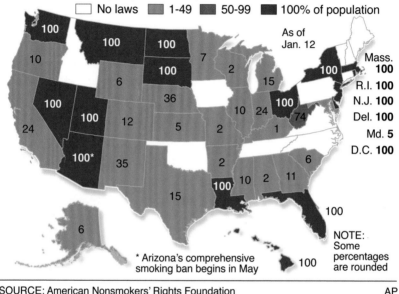

☐ No laws ▩ 1-49 ▩ 50-99 ■ 100% of population

As of Jan. 12

Mass. **100**
R.I. **100**
N.J. **100**
Del. **100**
Md. **5**
D.C. **100**

NOTE: Some percentages are rounded

* Arizona's comprehensive smoking ban begins in May

SOURCE: American Nonsmokers' Rights Foundation   AP

Smoking bans in the workplace have become more and more common throughout the country. The graphic above shows, in percentages, how many people in each state are affected by smoking bans in their workplaces.

exacerbated by his employer's refusal to enforce its existing no-smoking policy. A lower court had dismissed the employee's suit because the employee failed to present scientific evidence concerning the harmful effects of secondhand smoke. The appeals court reversed this decision, noting that the employer did not dispute that secondhand smoke is harmful. The court wrote, "While the duty to provide a reasonably safe workplace may not always be breached by the presence of secondhand smoke, we cannot accept the proposition that it can never be breached by an employer's failure to abate secondhand cigarette smoke in the workplace that aggravates a plaintiff's existing lung disease."[16]

Smoking bans should be imposed in other public places.

Many courts have upheld state and local clean indoor air laws or antismoking regulations. Some states began passing antismoking legislation in the 1970s. Arizona passed such a law in 1973. It banned smoking in many public places, including elevators, libraries, theaters, and buses. In 1975, Minnesota passed its State Clean Indoor Air Act, which prohibited smoking in many public places and workplaces. Today, most states have passed so-called clean indoor air laws to limit smoking in public places. These laws generally restrict, or even ban entirely, smoking in many public places. They often allow smoking only in certain designated areas.

In *City of Tucson v. Grezaffi*, an Arizona appeals court upheld a city law limiting smoking in restaurants.[17] The ordinance generally provided that "all restaurants shall be smoke-free." The ordinance made it unlawful for restaurant operators or managers to allow smoking in restaurants except for in designated smoking areas, or to "allow smoke from a designated smoking area to diffuse or drift into a non-smoking area." A group of restaurant owners challenged the constitutionality of the ordinance on several grounds. They argued, for instance, that the law infringed on the First Amendment right of freedom of association, violated the equal protection clause by singling out restaurants, and could be categorized as an unconstitutional "special" law (legislation that applies to a particular class or person). The appeals court determined that all of these constitutional challenges were meritless.

Since 1990, the federal government has eliminated smoking on nearly all domestic flights. Federal law provides: "An individual may not smoke in an aircraft in scheduled passenger interstate

FROM THE BENCH

Shimp v. New Jersey Bell Telephone Company, 145 N.J. Super. 516, 368 A.2d 408 (1976)

Employer's refusal to enact work place smoking ban denies nonsmoking employee who is severely allergic to gases produced by burning cigarettes her common-law right to safe working environment.

This case involves a matter of first impression in New Jersey: whether a nonsmoking employee is denied a safe working environment and is entitled to injunctive relief when forced by proximity to smoking employees to involuntarily inhale "secondhand" cigarette smoke. The nonsmoking employee has severe allergic reaction to cigarette smoke. She alleges that her employer, the N.J. Bell Telephone Company, is causing her to work in an unsafe environment by refusing to ban smoking in the office where she is employed.

It is clearly the law of New Jersey that an employee has the right to work in a safe environment. An employer is under an affirmative duty to provide a work area that is free from unsafe conditions. This right to safe and healthful working conditions is protected not only by the duty imposed by common law upon employers but also by the Occupational Safety and Health Act, 29 U.S.C. §§651–78. OSHA in no way preempts the field of occupational safety. 29 U.S.C. §653(b) (4) recognizes concurrent state power to act either legislatively or judicially under common law with regard to occupational safety.

The nonsmoking employee has a common-law right to a safe working environment. The issue remains whether the work area here is unsafe due to a preventable hazard that the court may enjoin. There can be no doubt that the byproducts of burning tobacco are toxic and dangerous to the health of smokers and nonsmokers generally, and to this employee in particular.

The national policy to warn the public of the dangerous nature of cigarette smoke, as expressed in the Public Health Cigarette Smoking Act, 15 U.S.C. §§1331 et seq., has made that fact generally acceptable. The court takes judicial notice of the toxic nature of cigarette smoke and its well-known association with emphysema, lung cancer, and heart disease.

air transportation or scheduled passenger intrastate air transportation."[18] This rule was not always the case. In fact, in 1971,
a federal appeals court rejected a claim by consumer advocate

---

The HEW Report for 1975, The Health Consequences of Smoking, indicates that the more presence of cigarette smoke in the air pollutes it, changing carbon monoxide levels and effectively making involuntary smokers of all who breathe air. Prior to this report, it was generally accepted that smoking is a hazard voluntarily undertaken. The opinion that tobacco smoke should be eliminated from the work environment is shared by allergists, immunologists and specialists in the field of industrial medicine.

The evidence is clear and overwhelming. Cigarette smoke contaminates and pollutes the air creating a health hazard not merely to the smoker but to all those around the smoker who must rely upon the same air supply. The right of an individual to risk his or her own health does not include the right to jeopardize the health of those who must remain around him or her in order to properly perform the duties of their jobs. The portion of the population that is especially sensitive to cigarette smoke is so significant that it is reasonable to expect an employer to foresee health consequences and to impose upon the employer a duty to abate the hazard causing the discomfort.

The employees' right to a safe working environment makes it clear that smoking must be forbidden in the work area. The employee who desires to smoke on his or her own time, during coffee breaks and lunch hours, should have a reasonably accessible area to smoke. Such a rule imposes no hardship upon the telephone company.

The company already has in effect a rule that cigarettes are not to be smoked around telephone equipment. The rationale behind the rule is that the machines are extremely sensitive and can be damaged by the smoke. Human beings are also very sensitive and can be damaged by cigarette smoke. Unlike a piece of machinery, the damage to a human is all too often irreparable. If a circuit or wiring goes bad, the company can install a replacement part. It is not so simple in the case of a human lung, eye, or heart. The parts are hard to come by, if indeed they can be found at all. A company that has demonstrated such concern for its mechanical components should have at least as much concern for its human beings.

Ralph Nader challenging smoking on aircraft flights. The court responded that the freedom to smoke had been "enjoyed by millions of passengers since the advent of commercial aviation" and that "the freedom to smoke may have to give way to the freedom of others to be unannoyed by smoke but that is not a safety problem."[19]

THE LETTER OF THE LAW

Florida Clean Indoor Air Act: 2003 FL H.B. 63

Be It Enacted by the Legislature of the State of Florida:

Section 2. Section 386.202, Florida Statutes, is amended to read:

386.202 Legislative intent.—The purpose of this part is to protect people from the public health hazards of secondhand tobacco smoke and to implement the Florida health initiative in s. 20, Art. X of the State Constitution. It is the intent of the Legislature to discourage the designation of any area within a government building as a smoking area....

Section 4. Section 386.204, Florida Statutes, is amended to read:

386.204 Prohibition.—A person may not smoke in an enclosed indoor workplace, except as otherwise provided in s. 386.2045.

Section 5. Section 386.2045, Florida Statutes, is created to read:

386.2045 Enclosed indoor workplaces; specific exceptions.—Notwithstanding s.386.204, tobacco smoking may be permitted in each of the following places:

(1) PRIVATE RESIDENCE.—A private residence whenever it is not being used commercially to provide child care, adult care, or health care, or any combination thereof as defined in s.386.203(1).
(2) RETAIL TOBACCO SHOP—An enclosed indoor workplace dedicated to or predominantly for the retail sale of tobacco, tobacco products, and accessories for such products, as defined in s.386.203(8).
(3) DESIGNATED SMOKING GUEST ROOM.—A designated smoking guest room at a public lodging establishment as defined in s.386.203(4).

More cities are regulating smoking in a variety of public places, such as restaurants, bars, public parks, and sidewalks. San Francisco bans smoking in city parks and on golf courses. The push to regulate smoking now extends beyond public places to the home. Many courts are looking at smoking as a factor in custody determinations between parents. One commentator

---

(4) STAND-ALONE BAR.—A business that meets the definition of a stand-alone bar as defined in s.386.203(11) and that otherwise complies with all applicable provisions of the Beverage Law and part II of this chapter.

...

Section 7. Section 386.206, Florida Statutes, is amended to read:

386.206 Posting of signs; requiring policies.—

(1) The person in charge of an enclosed indoor workplace that prior to adoption of s. 20, Art. X of the State Constitution was required to post signs under the requirements of this section must continue to conspicuously post, or cause to be posted, signs stating that smoking is not permitted in the enclosed indoor workplace. Each sign posted pursuant to this section must have letters of reasonable size which can be easily read. The color, design, and precise place of posting of such signs shall be left to the discretion of the person in charge of the premises....

Section 12. Section 386.212, Florida Statutes, is reenacted and amended to read:

386.212 Smoking prohibited near school property; penalty.—

(1) It is unlawful for any person under 18 years of age to smoke tobacco in, on, or within 1,000 feet of the real property comprising a public or private elementary, middle, or secondary school between the hours of 6 a.m. and midnight. This section does not apply to any person occupying a moving vehicle or within a private residence....

This act shall take effect July 1, 2003.

writes: "When a child's environment subjects him or her to harm through the inhalation of dangerous substances, precautionary measures should not only be taken into account but regulated to ensure the child's best interests are met."[20]

Law professor David Ezra argues in a 2001 law review article that "current law allows landlords, property managers, and homeowners associations to restrict or eliminate smoking, even in the friendly confines of one's own home."[21] He cites a Utah state law that allows condominium associations to declare tobacco smoking a nuisance.

Smoking bans should apply to prisons.

The movement to limit ETS exposure has even been extended to prisons. In 1993, the U.S. Supreme Court ruled in *Helling v.*

FROM THE BENCH

City of Tucson v. Grezaffi, 23 P.3d 675 (Ariz. App. 2001)

Restaurant owner was held responsible by magistrate for violation of city's restaurant smoking ordinance, and restaurant owner appealed.... The Court of Appeals, Pelander, J., held that: (1) review was limited to whether ordinance was constitutional on its face; (2) city had authority under city charter to promulgate ordinance banning smoking in restaurants; (3) ordinance was not preempted by state statutes....

City ordinance that promoted public welfare by prohibiting smoking in restaurants was a rational, legitimate means of safeguarding the general health, safety, and welfare of the community and did not violate restaurant owner's equal protection rights, though ordinance did not apply to other establishments, such as bars, bowling alleys or billiard halls....

In October 1999, Grezaffi was cited on a civil infraction for having violated Code §11–19 (E) (2) which ... prohibits restaurant owners from allowing persons to smoke in restaurants except in a designated smoking area and from allowing smoke to diffuse or drift from a designated smoking area into a nonsmoking area. After an evidentiary hearing, a Tucson City Court magistrate found Grezaffi responsible, imposed a fine or community service, and ordered her to abate the violation....

McKinney that an inmate could sue prison officials for exposure to ETS.[22] William McKinney, a Nevada inmate, sued prison officials after they placed him in a cell with another inmate who smoked five packs of cigarettes a day. McKinney alleged that the prison officials subjected him to cruel and unusual punishment in violation of the Eighth Amendment by forcing him to live with a smoker. He contended that prison officials were showing deliberate indifference to his health by intentionally exposing him to high levels of ETS.

Prison officials countered that McKinney could not sue them for any future harm the exposure to smoke might cause him because any such harm would be speculative. They said that McKinney could not recover damages unless he could show

Contrary to Grezaffi's contention, we have no difficulty concluding that the ordinance is "rationally and reasonably related to furthering some legitimate governmental interest." ... Significant scientific evidence suggests that smoking or exposure to secondhand smoke poses serious and substantial health risks. Grezaffi does not contest that proposition. Because the ordinance's goal of promoting the public welfare by alleviating smoke-related health concerns in restaurants is self-evident, "we need look no further." ... The ordinance unquestionably is a reasonable, legitimate means of "safeguarding the general health, safety, and welfare of the community." ...

[T]he ordinance bears a rational relationship to a legitimate, legislative purpose: preservation of the citizenry's health, comfort, safety, and welfare. Second, the ordinance applies "uniformly to all cases and to all members within the circumstances provided for by the law," that is, to all restaurants within the city.... Third, the ordinance is elastic because it permits restaurants to enter or exit its coverage depending on whether they have or no longer have certain specified characteristics. All restaurants in Tucson must comply with the ordinance's requirements....

All of Grezaffi's constitutional challenges to the City's restaurant smoking ordinance are without merit. Code §11–19 is facially valid. Accordingly, the superior court's order denying Grezaffi's appeal is affirmed.

that he was currently suffering serious medical problems associated with exposure to tobacco smoke. The Court rejected that argument, writing: "It would be odd to deny an injunction to inmates who plainly proved an unsafe, life-threatening condition in their prison on the ground that nothing yet had happened to them."[23]

Some correctional institutions responded to this decision by banning smoking in their prisons. Some inmates sued the prison officials, contending that the smoking bans violated their constitutional rights. One federal court in Maryland ruled that state prison officials, in light of the Supreme Court's decision in *Helling*, could ban smoking. "It should be perfectly

THE LETTER OF THE LAW

From the Legislature: Utah Code Ann. Section 78-38-5, 78-38-1

78-38-5 Legislative intent.

(1) The Legislature finds:
   (a) the federal Environmental Protection Agency (EPA) has determined that environmental tobacco smoke is a Group A carcinogen, in the same category as other cancer-causing chemicals such as asbestos....
(2) The Legislature finds that environmental tobacco smoke generated in a rental or condominium unit may drift into other units, exposing the occupants of those units to tobacco smoke, and that standard construction practices are not effective in preventing this drift of tobacco smoke.
(3) The Legislature further finds that persons who desire to not be exposed to drifting environmental tobacco smoke should be able to determine in advance of entering into a rental, lease, or purchase agreement whether the subject unit may be exposed to environmental tobacco smoke.

obvious to any rational person that the State of Maryland, in view of the well-known harmful effects of secondhand smoke, has a legitimate interest in protecting the health of nonsmokers forced to be its guests in correctional facilities," the court wrote. "In fact, the Supreme Court has held that state actors could face liability under section 1983 if they do not protect nonsmokers from smokers' secondhand smoke."[24]

Summary

A significant body of scientific evidence—from both the public and private sectors—establishes that exposure to environmental tobacco smoke presents serious health hazards for nonsmokers.

78–38–1 Nuisance defined—Right of action for—Judgment.

(1) A nuisance is anything which is injurious to health, indecent, offensive to the senses, or an obstruction to the free use of property, so as to interfere with the comfortable enjoyment of life or property. A nuisance may be the subject of an action.

(2) A nuisance may include the following:
   (a) drug houses and drug dealing ...
   (b) gambling ...

(3) A nuisance under this section includes tobacco smoke that drifts into any residential unit a person rents, leases, or owns, from another residential or commercial unit and this smoke:
   (a) drifts in more than once in each of two or more consecutive seven-day periods; and

(9) A cause of action for a nuisance under Subsection (3) may be brought against:
   (a) the individual generating the tobacco smoke;
   (b) the renter or lessee who permits or fails to control the generation of tobacco smoke, in violation of the terms of his rental or lease agreement, on the premises he rents or leases ...

This evidence also establishes that ETS exposure presents severe risks for children. Since the 1970s, society has increasingly recognized the rights of nonsmokers through a variety of measures. State and local legislators have passed a series of clean indoor air laws. Several courts have recognized that employers have a

FROM THE BENCH

Helling v. McKinney, 509 U.S. 25 (1993)

Respondent McKinney, a Nevada state prisoner, filed suit against petitioner prison officials, claiming that his involuntary exposure to environmental tobacco smoke (ETS) from his cellmate's and other inmates' cigarettes posed an unreasonable risk to his health, thus subjecting him to cruel and unusual punishment in violation of the Eighth Amendment. A federal magistrate granted petitioners' motion for a directed verdict, but the Court of Appeals reversed in part, holding that McKinney should have been permitted to prove that his ETS exposure was sufficient to constitute an unreasonable danger to his future health. It reaffirmed its decision after this Court remanded for further consideration in light of *Wilson v. Seiter*, 501 U.S. 294, in which the Court held that Eighth Amendment claims arising from confinement conditions not formally imposed as a sentence for a crime require proof of a subjective component, and that, where the claim alleges inhumane confinement conditions or failure to attend to a prisoner's medical needs, the standard for that state of mind is the "deliberate indifference" standard of *Estelle v. Gamble*, 429 U.S. 97. The Court of Appeals held that Seiter's subjective component did not vitiate that court's determination that it would be cruel and unusual punishment to house a prisoner in an environment exposing him to ETS levels that pose an unreasonable risk of harming his health—the objective component of McKinney's claim.

Held:
1. It was not improper for the Court of Appeals to decide the question whether McKinney's claim could be based on possible future effects of ETS. From its examination of the record, the court was apparently of the view that the claimed entitlement to a smoke-free environment subsumed the claim that ETS exposure could endanger one's future, not just current, health.
2. By alleging that petitioners have, with deliberate indifference, exposed him to ETS levels that pose an unreasonable risk to his future health,

duty to protect nonsmoking employees from health hazards associated with smokers. The U.S. Supreme Court weighed in on the issue in a prisoner civil rights case, refusing to dismiss a lawsuit by a prisoner who alleged that he was facing potential health threats by being subjected to high levels of ETS. In the

McKinney has stated an Eighth Amendment claim on which relief could be granted. An injunction cannot be denied to inmates who plainly prove an unsafe, life-threatening condition on the ground that nothing yet has happened to them.... Thus, petitioners' central thesis that only deliberate indifference [509 U.S. 25, 26] to inmates' current serious health problems is actionable is rejected. Since the Court cannot at this juncture rule that McKinney cannot possibly prove an Eighth Amendment violation based on ETS exposure, it also would be premature to base a reversal on the Federal Government's argument that the harm from ETS exposure is speculative, with no risk sufficiently grave to implicate a serious medical need, and that the exposure is not contrary to current standards of decency. On remand, the District Court must give McKinney the opportunity to prove his allegations, which will require that he establish both the subjective and objective elements necessary to prove an Eighth Amendment violation. With respect to the objective factor, he may have difficulty showing that he is being exposed to unreasonably high ETS levels, since he has been moved to a new prison and no longer has a cellmate who smokes, and since a new state prison policy restricts smoking to certain areas and makes reasonable efforts to respect nonsmokers' wishes with regard to double bunking. He must also show that the risk of which he complains is not one that today's society chooses to tolerate. The subjective factor, deliberate indifference, should be determined in light of the prison authorities' current attitudes and conduct, which, as evidenced by the new smoking policy, may have changed considerably since the Court of Appeals' judgment. The inquiry into this factor also would be an appropriate vehicle to consider arguments regarding the realities of prison administration.

959 F.2d 853, affirmed and remanded.

last 10 years, courts have determined that smoking is a relevant factor in child custody decisions. There is also now a movement to limit smoking in multi-unit residences, such as apartment buildings and condominiums.

The movement for smoking bans is having a positive impact, as more and more people quit smoking. Some studies have shown that after smoking bans go into effect, there is a reduction in the sales of cigarettes. California, for example, has experienced a steady reduction in smoking since its first anti-smoking law in 1988.[25] A study of smokers in Lexington, Kentucky, showed that the city's percentage of adult smokers dropped by nearly one-third since an indoor smoking ban was implemented in April 2004.[26]

The writing is on the wall: Smoking bans are legal and necessary. As legal commentator Samuel Winokur writes, "The only effective means of protecting nonsmokers in a public place is a smoking ban."[27]

Smoking Bans Infringe on Smokers' Individual Rights

Indeed, the [smoking] bans are symptoms of a far more grievous threat, a cancer that has been spreading for decades and has now metastasized throughout the body politic, spreading even to the tiniest organs of local government. This cancer is the only real hazard involved—the cancer of unlimited government power.

—Columnist Robert W. Tracinski[1]

In England in 2001, 41-year-old sales executive Mark Hodges was fired on the second day of his job because his company had instituted a no-smoking policy for employees. Although Hodges had been informed of the policy when he interviewed for the position, he said he had assumed that it was in effect only when he was at the office or in his company car. Hodges had not smoked in either of these places. He had smoked at home.

As Hodges explained, "I was sacked for smoking in my free time. I am angry and astounded I could be treated like that." In response to the incident, Ben Williams, a spokesperson for the British smokers' rights group Forest, said, "We know of cases in the U.S. where employees have been breathalysed when they got to work. This is a very extreme case but it does serve as an example [of where] cases may go in the future."[2]

Many legal activities in society are dangerous: riding a motorcycle, skydiving, eating fatty foods, and even working too hard. In a free society, individuals are given the choice to engage in a variety of activities that may not be the best decision. Some people believe that state restrictions on smoking amount to a form of "legal paternalism" that infringes on the fundamental right to liberty enshrined in the Declaration of Independence.[3]

The rush to regulate tobacco has drawn comparisons to the era of Prohibition, when the Eighteenth Amendment to the U.S. Constitution banned the making and selling of alcohol. "Ultimately some of the worst social costs come not from drinking or smoking, but from the enormous social, political, economic, and moral consequences of going too far in limiting behavior," writes Mark Edward Lender in his article "The New Prohibition."[4] Prohibition proved to be a complete failure, as people continued to consume alcohol. It seems that the same is happening with cigarettes. People will continue to smoke no matter what regulations are put into place.

The EPA study on secondhand smoke is questionable.

Sidney Zion in his article "Science and Secondhand Smoke" writes: "There is nothing more powerful than a lie whose time has come. Thus, the smoking bans."[5] Some studies have questioned whether environmental tobacco smoke causes heart disease or lung cancer. One 1998 study from the *Journal of the National Cancer Institute* concluded that there was not a statistically significant connection between exposure to secondhand smoke and lung cancer: "Our results indicate no association between childhood exposure to ETS and lung cancer risk. We did find weak evidence of a dose–response relationship between risk of lung cancer and exposure to spousal and workplace ETS. There was no detectable risk after cessation of exposure."[6] According to tobacco giant R.J. Reynolds:

> An individual's risk for contracting a smoking-related disease is based on many factors in addition to smoking.... Considering all of the evidence, in our opinion, it seems unlikely that secondhand smoke presents any significant harm to otherwise healthy nonsmoking adults at the very low concentrations commonly encountered in homes, offices, and other places where smoking is allowed.[7]

When the EPA issued its report classifying secondhand smoke as a carcinogen that was responsible for causing 3,000 deaths per year, several tobacco companies challenged the report in a federal lawsuit. The companies argued that the EPA failed to follow proper procedure and altered its methodology to reach a desired result. According to the tobacco companies, the EPA also wrongfully failed to include a tobacco industry representative on the advisory committee for the study.

In 1999, federal district court judge William Osteen agreed with the tobacco companies in *Flue-Cured Tobacco Cooperative Stabilization Corporation v. United States Environmental Protection Agency*.[8] He found there was substantial evidence that the EPA had "cherry-picked" among various studies and altered its own standards to reach a certain result. "Using its normal methodology and its selected studies, EPA did not demonstrate a statistically significant association between ETS and lung cancer," Judge Osteen wrote. "Instead, EPA changed its methodology to find a statistically significant association."[9] Osteen concluded that the "EPA's conduct left substantial holes in the administrative record" and that "EPA produced limited evidence, then claimed the weight of the Agency's research evidence demonstrated ETS causes cancer.[10]

A federal appeals court reversed Judge Osteen's decision but did not dispute his findings. The appeals court determined that the tobacco companies could not challenge the EPA's report in federal court because the federal court did not have jurisdiction over an agency report that was not "final agency action" within the meaning of federal administrative law. This is because courts generally cannot review administrative actions until the full administrative process has taken place. However, even the federal appeals court seemed disturbed by the EPA's conduct, writing that "exclusion by the EPA of any meaningful tobacco industry representative from the advisory committee . . . is unexplained."[11]

The controversy over the EPA's handling of its report about secondhand smoke caused one commentator to write: "Despite the rhetoric of the anti-tobacco industry, science does not back up the ETS scare campaign."[12]

Many smoking bans were passed without proper authority.

Many cities and counties have passed smoking bans even when they did not possess the authority to do so. In 2003, a legal dispute brewed in the state of New York over a law that bans smoking in many public places, including bars. A group of bar associations, led by the Empire State Restaurant and Tavern Association, sued the state, contending that the law was unconstitutional.

In *Empire State Restaurant and Tavern Association v. New York State*, the plaintiffs alleged that the smoking ban violates due process, is preempted by federal law, and violates the supremacy clause of the U.S. Constitution. They further contended that the New York state law is preempted by the federal regulations of the Occupational Safety and Health Administration (OSHA) on worker exposure to tobacco smoke. In their complaint, they argue that the New York law's "broad ban on smoking in workplaces directly, substantially and specifically regulates occupational safety and health."[13]

Smoking slowly being rubbed out

New Jersey is the newest state to join a growing number of others to place a ban on smoking. Currently, there are 17 states with no-smoking laws in effect, along with 461 towns, cities and counties.

State no-smoking laws

Banned in all workplaces, restaurants and bars

Banned in either workplaces, restaurants or bars

• Locality with a no-smoking law

Mass.

N.J.

Del.

D.C.

SOURCE: Americans for Nonsmokers' Rights   AP

In the name of public health, more states and municipalities are banning smoking in public places, including restaurants, bars, and workplaces. Some states have bans covering all three. The map above shows which states and cities had bans in place as of 2006.

Empire State argued that the federal law under OSHA pre-empts or trumps state law. Because the New York law regulates an area under federal control, the plaintiffs argued that it violates the supremacy clause of the Constitution, which provides that the federal laws of the United States "shall be the supreme Law of the Land." A federal district court judge refused to enjoin or stop enforcement of the law in October 2003, but the lawsuit continues.

The Ohio supreme court recently ruled that a county board of health exceeded its authority when it passed a smoking ban. Such authority, reasoned the court, resided with the state legislature— not an administrative agency like the local health board. The court stated: "There is no express grant of power [in the state law] or elsewhere, allowing local boards of health unfettered authority to promulgate any health regulation deemed necessary."[14]

The phenomenon prompted South Carolina State Senator John Graham Altman III to introduce a bill in June 2003 that would prohibit cities from passing smoking bans in restaurants and bars. The bill, which did not pass, would have provided that cities that ignored this provision would risk losing state funding. "This is an issue of government becoming more and more socialistic and telling the owners and operators of private property what they can and can't do," Altman told a Charleston newspaper.[15]

State smoking bans are not insulated from legal attacks either. The Empire State Restaurant and Tavern Association has challenged the constitutionality of New York's state indoor smoking ban. Besides the question of constitutionality, the enforcement of the law has had a devastating financial impact on many taverns and bars. Another effect of the state law will be to force more smoking onto public streets, increasing the exposure to smoke for people walking the streets.

Some local officials have even sought to extend their local smoking bans to purely private establishments. In a Massachusetts case, city officials sought to enforce their smoking ban on a fraternal lodge. A state appeals court rejected the extension of the smoking ban on the lodge, a private establishment to which the general public did not have access.[16]

In October 2003, the West Virginia state supreme court heard arguments in a case that challenged a county smoking ban. The court will decide whether the state legislature gave county health boards the authority to regulate secondhand smoke. The county argues that the legislature gave the county health boards the power to regulate clean air and water, which includes the ability to regulate secondhand smoke. Lawyers for those challenging the ban contend that the county health boards do not have the power to regulate tobacco.[17] Also in October 2003, the Montana supreme court agreed to review a case challenging the validity of smoking bans in that state. These court decisions could eventually lead to a challenge before the U.S. Supreme Court.

THE LETTER OF THE LAW

From the Tennessee and South Dakota Legislatures

Tennessee: T.C.A. 50–1-304(e)
No employee shall be discharged or terminated solely for participating or engaging in the use of an agricultural product not regulated by the alcoholic beverage commission that is not otherwise proscribed by law, if such employee participates or engages in such use in a manner which complies with all applicable employer policies regarding such use during times at which such employee is working.

South Dakota 60–4-11 Discrimination against employee's off-duty use of tobacco
It is a discriminatory or unfair employment practice for an employer to terminate the employment of an employee due to that employee's engaging in any use of tobacco products off the premises of the employer during nonworking hours unless such a restriction:

(1) Relates to a bona fide occupational requirement and is reasonably and rationally related to the employment activities and responsibilities of a particular employee or a particular group of employees, rather than to all employees of the employer; or

(2) Is necessary to avoid a conflict of interest with any responsibilities to the employer or the appearance of such a conflict of interest.

Workers who smoke face discrimination.

The majority of states have passed laws prohibiting employers from firing workers who smoke while off duty or on breaks in specifically designated smoking areas. Such laws protect workers who follow the employer's guidelines about when and where they can smoke while on duty. It also ensures that employers do not invade the private lives of their employees by regulating off-duty behavior.

The Indiana Court of Appeals ruled that an employee was entitled to unemployment compensation when his employer fired him for violating a company rule prohibiting drinking and smoking while off duty. The employee had allegedly drunk a beer at a bar while not on the job. The court wrote, "in order for an employer rule which regulates an employee's off-duty activity to be considered reasonable, the activity sought to be regulated must bear some reasonable relationship to the employer's business interest."[18]

Summary

It has been established that smoking is bad for smokers. Many activities in life are dangerous or unhealthy, including various types of food and recreational activities. But the United States is a free society. If the government is allowed unlicensed and unchecked authority to regulate private choices, people will no longer be living in an age of individual responsibility. And, although it has been proven that smoking cigarettes can cause cancer, the case against secondhand smoke has been scientifically questionable. Some studies have found little, if any, statistical association between secondhand smoke and lung cancer. A federal judge ruled that the Environmental Protection Agency's 1993 report classifying secondhand smoke as a carcinogen was deeply flawed.

The push for smoking bans infringes on individual freedom of choice. Extending smoking bans to bars and outdoor establishments shows that society has now crossed the line toward discrimination against smokers. Many states have had to pass anti–smoking-discrimination laws to protect smokers from outright discrimination in the workforce. The rush to ban smoking has had a detrimental economic impact on many businesses. Bars, restaurants, and even casinos have been hurt by such bans.[19]

The attack against smoking—however well intentioned—has gone too far. Dr. Michael Siegel, one of the leaders of the original antismoking movement, says that the movement has strayed from its original purpose. "The goal was to get rid of smoking in the workplace," he has said. "I never understood that the goal was to get rid of smoking so that no one even gets a whiff of smoke."[20] The antismoking crusade runs the risk of becoming a full-fledged modern-day Prohibition—a policy of the early twentieth century that is viewed with contempt. One columnist expressed it well: "Today, Big Brother is after smokers. Tomorrow, will it sanction social drinkers, overeaters, or people who wear pink? Where does the 'government nannyism' end? In this classic clash between individual rights and public welfare, government just ought to butt out."[21]

Suits Against Big Tobacco Are Legitimate Cases Against Wealthy Defendants Selling Harmful Products

I n 1999, a California jury awarded 52-year-old Patricia Henley a $51.5-million verdict after Henley sued Philip Morris for deliberately misrepresenting the dangers of smoking. Prior to being diagnosed with terminal lung cancer, Henley had smoked three packs of cigarettes a day since she began to smoke as a teenager. In response to the verdict, Henley said, "I feel wonderful. I went into this case figuring we'd never beat big business." She said that she intended to donate her damages money to help educate children about the risks of smoking.[1]

Tobacco industry executives oversee a billion-dollar industry that causes horrible health hazards for its consumers. Tobacco producers have engaged in a pattern of deceitful behavior, concealing the level of harmfulness and addictiveness of their product. They have aggressively marketed this unreasonably dangerous product to the public. Lawsuits like Henley's have become more and more common over the past several years, and plaintiffs have often received enormous sums in their victories over the tobacco companies.

The basics of tort law allow anti-tobacco suits.

In the U.S. legal system, injured persons can sue those people who harm them in a civil action, known as a tort. For instance, if person A punches person B in the face, causing damage, B can sue A for the tort of battery. (B can also file a criminal lawsuit, since battery may also be a crime.) The person suing is called the *plaintiff* and the person being sued is called the *defendant*. In a tort suit, the defendant is sometimes referred to as the *tortfeasor*.

There are three main categories of torts: (1) intentional torts; (2) torts of negligence; and (3) strict liability torts. Intentional torts are those in which the defendant intended to bring about a certain result. Battery—when the defendant deliberately strikes the plaintiff with the goal of causing injury—is an example of an intentional tort.

Negligence refers to engaging in socially unreasonable conduct. A defendant does not need to intend to harm a victim in order to be negligent. For instance, if person A runs his car into person B's car, person A may be negligent and legally responsible even though he did not *intend* to hit the other car. Negligence cases require a plaintiff to prove duty (legal obligation), breach of

QUOTABLE

For 40 years, from 1954 to 1994, tobacco litigation provided the perfect example of David and Goliath litigation. Plaintiff after plaintiff was crushed by the tobacco defendants. Hundreds of claims were filed during those decades. The vast majority of the cases were dismissed before trial.
—Howard Erichson, Professor of Law, Seton Hall University

duty, causation, and damage. Often, the most challenging aspects of tort cases are proving breach of duty and causation. To show breach of duty, a plaintiff must demonstrate that the defendant acted unreasonably or failed to follow a particular standard of care. Causation requires the plaintiff to show that the defendant's conduct was the actual and legal cause of the plaintiff's injuries. Tobacco companies will often argue that tobacco products were not the legal cause of the plaintiff's harm. They may claim that the plaintiff's own conduct in purchasing the cigarettes, the plaintiff's own unhealthy eating habits, or the plaintiff's stressful work and home-life situations were the true causes of the plaintiff's health condition.

Finally, strict liability torts are those in which liability can be imposed without a showing of intent or negligence. Strict liability is sometimes used in products liability cases, where a defendant has introduced unreasonably dangerous products into the marketplace.

Regardless of the type of tort lawsuit, the most common remedy the plaintiff seeks is monetary damages. There are two main types of damages: compensatory damages and punitive damages. Compensatory damages are designed to pay back the plaintiff for the harm that he or she suffered. Punitive damages, on the other hand, seek to punish the wrongdoer.

One of the most challenging and fascinating aspects of tort law is its application to the tobacco companies. Individuals and states have sued tobacco companies under a variety of tort theories. For example, products liability suits have been filed, claiming that cigarettes are an unreasonably dangerous product. Other cases have argued that the tobacco companies were negligent in how they represented their product. Many lawsuits fault the tobacco companies for failing to warn consumers about known dangers. Litigation against tobacco companies also involves claims of failure to warn the public of health risks, conspiracy to conceal health information, and breach of express warranty.

Early plaintiffs failed to defeat the tobacco industry.

Beginning in the 1950s, smokers or their close relatives began suing the tobacco companies, claiming that the companies should be held liable for the harm that had befallen smokers. Experts have divided the periods of litigation against the tobacco industry into three eras: (1) 1954 to 1973, (2) 1983 to 1992, and (3) 1994 to the present. Plaintiffs in the first wave of litigation often lost their cases because their attorneys could not prove the causation between smoking and disease.

Even in the second wave of litigation, the tobacco industry successfully argued that the smokers themselves were also at fault, or contributorily negligent. Under the doctrine of contributory negligence, a plaintiff could not recover damages from a defendant if the plaintiff was also at fault. Only two-dozen suits were filed against the tobacco industry in the 1970s. Only one of those reached a jury, which ruled in favor of the tobacco companies.

Gradually, most states moved from the doctrine of contributory negligence to a system called comparative negligence. Under a system of comparative negligence, juries distribute the burden of fault among all parties. For example, a jury might find that a tobacco company was 50 percent at fault for injuries to a smoker, but that the smoker was also 50 percent at fault. The industry also relied on the assumption of risk doctrine. This concept holds that plaintiffs cannot sue for damages when they have knowingly taken part in a harmful activity.

In the third wave of litigation, however, new medical studies have provided nearly undeniable proof that smoking causes cancer. Also, more documents from the tobacco companies have established that the companies knew of the addictiveness of nicotine. The tobacco industry not only knew this, but it concealed its knowledge while making its products more addictive. This new information has led to more promising results for plaintiffs in the third wave of litigation. Law professor Richard L. Cupp Jr.

wrote that the new information about tobacco industry misconduct has turned the tide for plaintiffs and will likely lead to more
judgments in their favor.[2]

The *Cipollone* case sets a new standard.

In 1983, Rose Cipollone (a smoker since 1942) and her husband
sued several tobacco companies, seeking to have them pay for
damages she suffered from smoking. They sued for fraudulent
misrepresentation, conspiracy to deprive the public of needed
health information about cigarettes, failure to warn the public
about all health hazards, and breach of express warranty in company advertisements. The Cipollones' express warranty claim
was that the tobacco companies had "expressly warranted that
smoking the cigarettes which they manufactured and sold did
not present any significant health consequences."[3]

The tobacco companies argued that federal warning
statutes—the 1965 Federal Cigarette Labeling and Advertising Act
and the 1969 Public Health Cigarette Smoking Act—preempted
any state laws that had come about because of tort actions. The
warning label required by federal law read: "WARNING: THE SUR-
GEON GENERAL HAS DETERMINED THAT CIGARETTE SMOKING IS
DANGEROUS TO YOUR HEALTH." The companies argued that this
warning protected them from any lawsuits for conduct that took
place after the warning. A federal trial court rejected this preemption defense, but a federal appeals court accepted it. The
court of appeals reasoned that federal law "preempts those state
law damage actions relating to smoking and health that challenge
either the adequacy of the warning on cigarette packages or the
propriety of a party's actions with respect to the advertising and
promotion of cigarettes."

The case went back to the district court for trial. The district
court, following the reasoning of the court of appeals, dismissed
the claims of failure to warn, express warranty, fraudulent misrepresentation, and conspiracy to defraud claims. These allegations were barred for the most part because they relied on the

FROM THE BENCH

Cipollone v. Liggett Group, Inc., 505 U.S. 504 (1992)

Justice Stevens delivered the opinion of the Court.

Petitioner is the son of Rose Cipollone, who began smoking in 1942 and who died of lung cancer in 1984. He claims that respondents are responsible for Rose Cipollone's death because they breached express warranties contained in their advertising, because they failed to warn consumers about the hazards of smoking, because they fraudulently misrepresented those hazards to consumers, and because they conspired to deprive the public of medical and scientific information about smoking. The Court of Appeals held that petitioner's state-law claims were preempted by federal statutes, 893 F.2d 541 (CA3 1990), and other courts have agreed with that analysis. The highest court of the State of New Jersey, however, has held that the federal statutes [505 U.S. 504, 509] did not preempt similar common-law claims. Because of the manifest importance of the issue, we granted certiorari to resolve the conflict, 500 U.S. 499, 935 (1991). We now reverse in part and affirm in part....

We consider each category of damages actions in turn. In doing so, we express no opinion on whether these actions are viable claims as a matter of state law; we assume ... that they are.

Failure to Warn

To establish liability for a failure to warn, petitioner must show that "a warning is necessary to make a product ... reasonably safe, suitable and fit for its intended use," that respondents failed to provide such a warning, and that that failure was a proximate cause of petitioner's injury. In this case, petitioner offered two closely related theories concerning the failure to warn: first, that respondents "were negligent in the manner [that] they tested, researched, sold, promoted, and advertised" their cigarettes; and second, that respondents failed to provide "adequate warnings of the health consequences of cigarette smoking." App. 85–86.

Petitioner's claims are preempted to the extent that they rely on a state-law "requirement or prohibition ... with respect to ... advertising or promotion." Thus, insofar as claims under either failure-to-warn theory require a showing that respondents' post-1969 advertising or promotions should have included additional, or more clearly stated, warnings, those claims are preempted. The Act does not, however, preempt petitioner's claims that rely solely on respondents' [505 U.S. 504, 525] testing or research practices or other actions unrelated to advertising or promotion....

(continues)

(continued)

Fraudulent Misrepresentation

Petitioner alleges two theories of fraudulent misrepresentation. First, petitioner alleges that respondents, through their advertising, neutralized the effect of federally mandated warning labels. Such a claim is predicated on a state-law prohibition against statements in advertising and promotional materials that tend to minimize the health hazards associated with smoking. Such a prohibition, however, is merely the converse of a state-law requirement that warnings be included in advertising and promotional materials. Section 5(b) of the 1969 Act preempts both requirements and prohibitions; it therefore supersedes petitioner's first fraudulent misrepresentation theory.

Regulators have long recognized the relationship between prohibitions on advertising that downplays the dangers of smoking and requirements for warnings in advertisements. For example, the FTC, in promulgating its initial trade regulation rule in 1964, criticized advertising that "associated cigarette smoking with such positive attributes as contentment, glamour, romance, youth, happiness ... at the same time suggesting that smoking is an activity at least consistent with physical health and well-being." The Commission concluded:

> To avoid giving a false impression that smoking [is] innocuous, the cigarette manufacturer who represents the alleged pleasures or satisfactions of cigarette smoking in his advertising must also disclose the serious risks to life that smoking involves. 29 Fed. Reg. 8356 (1964)....

Conspiracy to Misrepresent or Conceal Material Facts

Petitioner's final claim alleges a conspiracy among respondents to misrepresent or conceal material facts concerning the health hazards of smoking. The predicate duty underlying this claim is a duty not to conspire to commit fraud....

To summarize our holding: the 1965 Act did not preempt state-law damages actions; the 1969 Act preempts petitioner's claims based on a failure to warn and the neutralization [505 U.S. 504, 531] federally mandated warnings to the extent that those claims rely on omissions or inclusions in respondents' advertising or promotions; the 1969 Act does not preempt petitioner's claims based on express warranty, intentional fraud and misrepresentation, or conspiracy.

The judgment of the Court of Appeals is accordingly reversed in part and affirmed in part, and the case is remanded for further proceedings consistent with this opinion.

tobacco companies' advertising activities after the federal warning labels had been introduced in 1965. However, the plaintiffs were allowed to proceed with some of their claims based on the tobacco companies' conduct before 1965. The trial lasted for four months. The jury awarded $400,000 to Rose Cipollone's husband (by then, Rose herself had died of lung cancer) but found Rose 80 percent responsible for her own injuries. Even so, the jury did award damages for the claim of loss of warranty.

Although the court of appeals affirmed the lower court's preemption rulings, it sent the case back for a new trial. The case was then appealed to the U.S. Supreme Court, which agreed to hear the case to resolve the preemption question.

The question before the court concerned the effect of Section 5(b) of the 1969 Public Health Cigarette Smoking Act. That provision stated: "No requirement or prohibition based on smoking and health shall be imposed under State law with respect to the advertising or promotion of any cigarettes the packages of which are labeled in conformity with the provisions of this Act." The Court determined that this provision preempted some of Cipollone's claims. It determined that her claim of failure to warn was preempted to the extent that the claim stated that the companies should have provided additional or more clearly worded warnings about the health hazards of cigarettes. However, the Court reasoned that the act did not preempt claims related solely to the companies' "testing or research practices or other actions unrelated to advertising or promotion."[4]

The Court further determined that federal law did not preempt Cipollone's claims of breach of warranty. The Court reasoned that federal law only preempts claims "imposed under State law." The Court held that there was no preemption because the tobacco company—not the state or its law—made the warranty. As the Court explained, "In short, a common-law remedy for a contractual commitment voluntarily undertaken should not be regarded as a 'requirement . . . imposed under State law' within the meaning" of federal law.[5]

The Court also determined that some of Cipollone's other claims, including her claims of conspiracy to misrepresent or conceal material facts, were not preempted. "Congress offered no sign that it wished to insulate cigarette manufacturers from long-standing rules governing fraud," the Court wrote.

FROM THE BENCH

Castano v. American Tobacco Co., 84 F. 3d 734 (5th Cir. 1996)

JERRY E. SMITH, Circuit Judge:

In what may be the largest class action ever attempted in federal court, the district court in this case embarked "on a road certainly less traveled, if ever taken at all," *Castano v. American Tobacco Co.*, 160 F.R.D. 544, 560 (E.D. La. 1995) (citing Edward C. Latham, *The Poetry of Robert Frost, "The Road Not Taken"* 105 (1969)), and entered a class certification order. The court defined the class as:

(a) All nicotine-dependent persons in the United States who have purchased and smoked cigarettes manufactured by the defendants;

(b) the estates, representatives, and administrators of these nicotine-dependent cigarette smokers; and

(c) the spouses, children, relatives and "significant others" of these nicotine-dependent cigarette smokers as their heirs or survivors....

This matter comes before us on interlocutory appeal, under 28 U.S.C. 1292(b), of the class certification order. Concluding that the district court abused its discretion in certifying the class, we reverse.

I.

A. The Class Complaint

The plaintiffs filed this class complaint against the defendant tobacco companies and the Tobacco Institute, Inc., seeking compensation solely for the injury of nicotine addiction.... The class compliant alleges nine causes of action: fraud and deceit, negligent misrepresentation, intentional infliction of emotional distress, negligence and negligent infliction of emotional distress, violation of state consumer protection statutes, breach of express warranty, breach of implied warranty, strict product liability, and redhibition pursuant to the Louisiana Civil Code.

The plaintiffs seek compensatory and punitive damages and attorneys' fees....

Private suits have continued against Big Tobacco.

In 1994, a group of plaintiffs' attorneys joined together to pursue a nationwide class-action lawsuit against the tobacco industry. The group, called the Castano group, spurred other sets of attorneys and advocates to join forces to face the mighty tobacco

The plaintiffs initially defined the class as "all nicotine dependent persons in the United States," including current, former and deceased smokers since 1943. Plaintiffs conceded that addiction would have to be proven by each class member; the defendants argued that proving class membership will require individual mini-trials to determine whether addiction actually exists....

II.

A district court must conduct a rigorous analysis of the rule 23 prerequisites before certifying a class.... The party seeking certification bears the burden of proof....

The district court erred in its analysis in two distinct ways. First, it failed to consider how variations in state law affect predominance and superiority. Second, its predominance inquiry did not include consideration of how a trial on the merits would be conducted.

Each of these defects mandates reversal....

In summary, whether the specter of millions of cases outweighs any manageability problems in this class is uncertain when the scope of any manageability problems is unknown. Absent considered judgment on the manageability of the class, a comparison to millions of individual trials is meaningless....

IV.

The district court abused its discretion by ignoring variations in state law and how a trial on the alleged causes of action would be tried. Those errors cannot be corrected on remand because of the novelty of the plaintiffs' claims. Accordingly, class treatment is not superior to individual adjudication.

We have once before stated that "traditional ways of proceeding reflect far more than habit. They reflect the very culture of the jury trial...." The collective wisdom of individual juries is necessary before this court commits the fate of an entire industry or, indeed, the fate of a class of millions, to a single jury. For the forgoing reasons, we REVERSE and REMAND with instructions that the district court dismiss the class complaint.

FROM THE BENCH

Burton v. R.J. Reynolds, 205 F.Supp. 1253 (D. Kan. 2002)

Plaintiff filed this personal injury products liability action against defendant R.J. Reynolds Tobacco Company ("Reynolds") claiming that defendant's cigarettes caused his peripheral vascular disease ("PVD") and addiction. Plaintiff asserted that Reynolds manufactured a defective product, failed to warn him that smoking causes addiction and PVD, negligently failed to test or research its product, fraudulently concealed the fact that smoking cigarettes causes addiction and PVD, and conspired with other members of the tobacco industry to fraudulently conceal the health effects of smoking....

Having considered all of the evidence introduced in the trial of this case and the additional evidence which was admitted at the hearing on punitive damages, as well as the papers filed by the parties and the arguments of counsel, the court is now prepared to issue its ruling concerning the amount to be awarded as punitive damages in this case. For the reasons set forth below, the court directs the Clerk of the Court to modify and amend the judgment previously entered in this case to award plaintiff punitive damages in the amount of $15,000,000....

Throughout this case the defendant vigorously proclaimed that smoking cigarettes is a choice, that people have been aware of its dangers for years, and that a person who smokes should be deemed to have assumed the risks associated with smoking. If Reynolds had made full disclosure, that argument would have great appeal in a free society. But, a free society where people are permitted to engage in conduct which may not always be beneficial or healthful to them depends on the manufacturers and purveyors of the products which people choose to consume being frank and open about the dangers of which they are aware in order to permit truly free choice. Here, the insidious nature of Reynolds' fraudulent concealment lies not only in the evidence of its bare failure to disclose vital information but also in the evidence of its campaign to obscure the public's ability to appreciate the risks of smoking by attacking the credibility of the public health community's concerns while at the same time withholding and ignoring evidence which was within its control that would have made the truth available to consumers....

Concealment of the addictive nature of nicotine in the context of the knowledge by Reynolds of its health-related dangers, including specifically the causal relationship with PVD, brought with it a high likelihood at the time of the misconduct that serious harm would arise. Here, of course, serious harm—very foreseeable serious harm—occurred to Mr. Burton. He became addicted to a product which he consumed to the point that it caused him to so lose circulation in his legs that they both had to be amputated. This factor weighs heavily against Reynolds. It did not deceive him about facts which might affect the value of a luxury automobile, for example. It engaged in misconduct which consisted of specifically withholding information about how seriously harmful the product is to the persons of those enticed to use it....

Reynolds is hugely profitable. Reynolds disclosed that it realized $505 million in net income in 2001, had over $1 billion in cash and cash equivalents and over $9 billion in stockholder equity. Plaintiff's expert testified that over the period from 1953 to 2001, Reynolds realized $34.6 billion in operating profit. While Reynolds presented expert testimony indicating that this figure was somewhat inflated because it included some profit from non-tobacco operations, an amount which Reynolds never quantified, and reflected operating profit instead of net income, there is no question that Reynolds reaped enormous profits from the sale of its cigarettes.

The court infers from the evidence that but for Reynold's misconduct, fewer people would have begun to smoke and those who had begun but desired to quit would have realized that the task might involve professional help. Knowledge that a product is not only risky to your health but also is addictive would seem to be a severe deterrent to consumption. The evidence does not permit a precise estimate of how many fewer cigarettes Reynolds would have sold had it been honest about the choice its potential consumers were asked to make. But, the vigor with which Reynolds pursued its campaign of concealment and obfuscation leads this court to the conclusion that the profitability of the misconduct was high....

[T]he sheer magnitude of Reynolds' wealth makes it imperative that the award be in an amount which is high enough to have at least some impact in order to carry out the statutory purposes of punishment and deterrence....

In this case, the jury awarded compensatory damages in the amount of $198,400. Using this figure, a $15 million punitive damage award creates a ratio of approximately 75 to 1. The court believes that such a ratio is appropriate given the extremely reprehensible nature of Reynolds' conduct....

IT IS THEREFORE ORDERED that the Clerk of the Court shall modify and amend the judgment previously entered in this case to award plaintiff punitive damages in the amount of $15,000,000.

industry. On March 29, 1994, in *Castano v. American Tobacco Co.*, more than 60 law firms sued the tobacco industry in a class-action lawsuit for the "injury of nicotine addiction."[6]

A federal appeals court decertified the multi-state class-action suit, pointing out that differences in state law and individual smokers made the case improper for a class-action suit: "The collective wisdom of individual juries is necessary before this court commits the fate of an entire industry or indeed, the fate of a class of millions, to a single jury."[7]

Since the late 1990s, however, several juries have tagged large tobacco companies with astronomical damage awards. These include punitive damage awards designed to punish the tobacco industry. The wealth of the defendant is taken into account when determining how much money to award the plaintiff or plaintiffs.

Plaintiffs seemed to have a better chance in tobacco cases once it was revealed—sometimes through whistleblowers (individuals who expose company wrongdoing)—that the tobacco industry actively concealed the danger and addictiveness of its products. One federal district court explained: "it is not for making a dangerous product that the defendant should be punished. It is for concealing how dangerous the product is that R.J. Reynolds merits punishment."[8]

In some cases, the tobacco industry has settled cases rather than risk a "runaway jury," or a jury that might impose enormous punitive damage awards. For example, in 1997, tobacco manufacturers agreed to pay $349 million to settle a class-action lawsuit filed in Florida on behalf of 60,000 flight attendants who claimed injuries from secondhand smoke on airplanes.

In 2002, the tobacco industry suffered some dramatic setbacks, including several huge punitive damage awards. These awards included one in *Bullock v. Philip Morris* for an astonishing $28 billion in punitive damages. A judge later reduced the award to $28 million. Another case resulted in a $150 million award, and a third verdict was for $37.5 million.[9]

The government has filed lawsuits, too.

Many suits filed against tobacco companies are either filed by individuals or are class-action lawsuits filed by groups of similarly situated individuals. But, in 1994, state governments got into the act of suing Big Tobacco.

In May 1994, the state of Mississippi became the first state to sue the tobacco industry to recover monies spent treating tobacco-caused illnesses. State Attorney General Mike Moore argued that the tobacco companies had committed conduct called "unjust enrichment" (receiving money through no effort of their own at the expense of another) and should be forced to compensate the state for its Medicaid costs due to tobacco-related illnesses. Law professor Howard Erichson writes that the government suits were a real breakthrough for two reasons: (1) state governments had the monetary resources to compete with the tobacco industry; and (2) the governmental suits avoided the classic argument advanced by the tobacco industry against individual smokers—individual responsibility (because this was a case of collective harm).[10]

The lawsuits filed by Mississippi, Minnesota, and several other states led the tobacco companies to agree to an unprecedented agreement in 1998 called the Master Settlement Agreement. The tobacco companies agreed to pay more than $200 billion to various states and would stop marketing their products to children in order to avoid future lawsuits by the states.

QUOTABLE

I believe they [the tobacco industry] are the most corrupt and evil corporate animal that has ever been created in this country's history. They sell a drug, they make a drug, and they sell it knowing that it's addictive. They market it to our children, who they know will become addicts and they know that they will die from causes attributable to tobacco-related disease.

—Mike Moore, Mississippi Attorney General

Summary

For decades, large, wealthy tobacco companies have made billions of dollars from individual consumers by selling cancer-causing products. Tobacco companies have long engaged in aggressive marketing campaigns encouraging the use of tobacco while concealing their full knowledge of the harmful and addictive nature of their products.

Tobacco companies should be subject to tort suits for their negligent and intentional conduct in the delivery of harmful products to the public. Although early tobacco suits may have laid much of the blame for people's health problems on individual responsibility, new evidence has shown just how addictive cigarettes are and how culpable the tobacco industry really is. The government has even pursued claims under the federal anti-racketeering law—called the Racketeer Influenced and Corrupt Organizations Act (RICO)—against tobacco companies. Although these cases are still working their way through the courts, early indications are that at least some of these efforts may prove fruitful. For example, in 2006 a federal district court ruled in *U.S. v. Philip Morris U.S.A.* that tobacco companies in the past had engaged in a plan to deceive the public about the danger and addictiveness of tobacco. The court deemed the details of that plan to be a violation of RICO.[11]

These developments have led to recent large verdicts against Big Tobacco. If a jury believes that a tobacco manufacturer did engage in a pattern of deception, then it is likely to issue a large award to the plaintiff. Many of the large punitive damage awards made in the last five to seven years have been reduced on appeal. Still, the possibility of being held liable for damages remains a frightening reality for the tobacco industry.

Suits Against Big Tobacco Ignore Personal Responsibility and Unfairly Demonize a Legal Activity

The price of one's freedom in a free society is responsibility for the consequences of one's actions. Liberty and responsibility are positively correlated. That's a fact. People who claim addiction causes people to smoke say the two are negatively correlated. That's fiction. We cannot increase freedom by decreasing personal responsibility. That's the road to serfdom.

—Jeffrey A. Schaler[1]

As cities across the United States continue to put public smoking bans into effect, some observers wonder what will happen to businesses that depended in various ways on tobacco. Not only have tobacco farmers and cigarette manufacturers suffered declines in profits, but smaller businesses, too, have begun to feel the effects. Particularly hard hit have been bars and restaurants where smoking was commonplace prior to the bans.

In September 2003, a report on New York City's smoking ban quoted restaurant owner Michelle Dell as saying, "The smoking ban has devastated my business. I may have to lay off workers soon. We need help before it's too late."[2]

At least since the 1960s, people have been aware of the health risks of smoking. The U.S. Surgeon General in 1964 issued a warning that smoking was a health hazard. Decades of warnings on cigarette packages, public service announcements (many funded by the tobacco companies themselves), and warnings from the medical profession have told individuals of the harms. People know that it causes lung cancer and other diseases and ailments. Nonetheless, in a free society, people have the right to choose whether or not to smoke.

Many juries reject plaintiffs' suits against Big Tobacco, reasoning that individuals know that cigarettes are harmful. Though the conduct of large tobacco companies has hardly been blameless, the companies do not force people to smoke. It is the individual who walks into a store and purchases the pack of cigarettes. "The campaign against cigarette manufacturers seeks to overturn the presumption of self-responsibility," writes one commentator. "What makes the case remarkable is that it potentially involves over a quarter of the total population of the U.S. and a product that has been legally sold for over 100 years."[3]

Many lawsuits against the tobacco industry claim that smokers' physical addiction to nicotine makes them smoke, and they are powerless to quit. Jeffrey Schaler writes of this argument: "Tobacco caused them to smoke, they claim, as if tobacco had a will of its own. . . . This doublespeak contradicts the scientific evidence: smokers quit all the time—when it is important for them to do so."[4]

Tobacco companies have provided ample warning about the dangers of smoking.

Some courts have ruled that tobacco companies do not have a duty to warn individuals of the harms of smoking because smoking is an obvious health hazard. In *Gibbs v. Republic Tobacco, L.P.*, a federal district court in Florida rejected the claims of a man who alleged he had been harmed by loose-leaf tobacco products (mainly chewing tobacco). The court wrote: "Courts throughout Florida have consistently and repeatedly held that there is no duty to warn consumers of the obvious dangers associated with certain products."[5] The court reasoned that the harm that may be caused by tobacco products was open and obvious.

A federal appeals court rejected the claim of a Tennessee man who sued a tobacco company after he contracted vascular disease. The man's doctors had testified that his cigarette smoking had caused the vascular disease. The man sued the tobacco company under the state's products liability statute. That law enables a person to sue for damages caused by "unreasonably dangerous" products. State law defined "unreasonably dangerous" as "dangerous to the extent beyond that which could be contemplated by the ordinary consumer who purchases it with the ordinary knowledge common to the community as to its characteristics." The court determined that cigarettes were not "unreasonably dangerous" because ordinary consumers should know of the risks and hazards. Tobacco has been used for more than 400 years and "knowledge that cigarette smoking is harmful to health is widespread and can be considered part of the common knowledge of the community."[6]

Similarly, a federal court in Alabama rejected the products liability claims of a state resident who sued a tobacco company for health problems caused by his smoking. The court said, "Without question, the federally mandated warning on packages of cigarettes for the last 30 years has adequately warned the public of the dangers of tobacco smoking."[7]

Some courts have gone farther, reasoning that consumers have known the risks of smoking since 1950 or earlier. In *Tompkins v. R.J. Reynolds Tobacco Company*, a federal court in New York ruled that the tobacco company's expert witness had

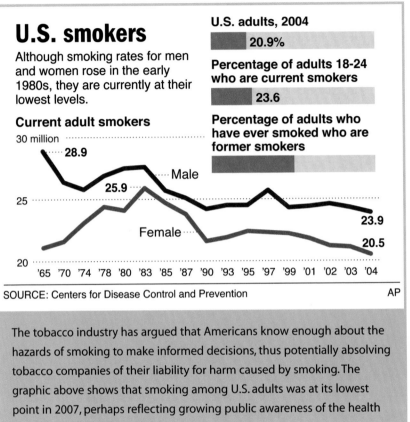

U.S. smokers

Although smoking rates for men and women rose in the early 1980s, they are currently at their lowest levels.

Current adult smokers

30 million

28.9

25.9

Male

25

Female

23.9

20.5

20

'65 '70 '74 '78 '80 '83 '85 '87 '90 '93 '95 '97 '99 '01 '02 '03 '04

U.S. adults, 2004

20.9%

Percentage of adults 18-24 who are current smokers

23.6

Percentage of adults who have ever smoked who are former smokers

SOURCE: Centers for Disease Control and Prevention   AP

The tobacco industry has argued that Americans know enough about the hazards of smoking to make informed decisions, thus potentially absolving tobacco companies of their liability for harm caused by smoking. The graphic above shows that smoking among U.S. adults was at its lowest point in 2007, perhaps reflecting growing public awareness of the health risks associated with cigarettes.

produced "overwhelming amounts of evidence showing a public awareness of the health risks of smoking since the turn of the twentieth century."[8] The court also questioned whether the plaintiff could show that the alleged failure of the tobacco company to warn the plaintiff of health hazards was the legal cause of his injuries, when the plaintiff presented no evidence that he truly would have quit had he really known of the dangers associated with smoking.

In another case, a court rejected a suit under a new tort called "intentional infliction of nicotine addiction." The court rejected the claim, stating that the plaintiff's attorney was not able to spell out the elements of such a novel cause of action when asked to do so in argument before the court. The plaintiff must provide notice to the defendant of the offense—"not a moving target," the court said.[9]

The plaintiff has a duty to prove causation.

A tort suit requires a plaintiff to prove (1) duty, (2) breach of duty, (3) causation, and (4) damages. The question of causation should prompt juries to closely examine the plaintiff's own lifestyle and bad habits. For instance, if a plaintiff died of heart disease, was it necessarily cigarette smoking that caused the death? The plaintiff may have had a family history of heart disease. He or she may also have experienced extreme job stress or a turbulent personal life. The plaintiff could have had other bad habits that led to the disease. For example, poor eating habits might just as easily have been the cause of the death.

Remember that a plaintiff has the burden of proof in a court case. The plaintiff must prove that cigarette smoking was the legal cause of his or her harm. Many times, there can be multiple causes of a particular event. If there are several different causes, then tobacco companies should not be forced to take total responsibility for the person's unfortunate situation. The plaintiff must present clear medical proof that smoking itself was the major factor in the harm.

Verdicts against Big Tobacco show that the tort system is in danger.

Some "runaway" juries have imposed verdicts of millions or billions of dollars against tobacco companies. This, according to some experts, clearly shows the need for tort reform. Critics believe that the tobacco verdicts award large sums of money to people whose harm was caused by their own bad choices.

One thing that tort reformers want to limit is punitive damages, the damages designed to punish the wrongdoer. Tort reform advocates argue that punitive damages offer a windfall to undeserving plaintiffs and drive up the cost of doing business. The U.S. Supreme Court has twice in the last decade ruled that punitive damage awards are allowed to be so high as to shock the conscience and violate the due process clause of the Fourteenth Amendment. In its 1996 decision in *BMW of North America, Inc.*

FROM THE BENCH

BMW of North America, Inc. v. Gore, 517 U.S. 559 (1996)

Justice Stevens delivered the opinion of the Court.

In January 1990, Dr. Ira Gore, Jr. (respondent), purchased a black BMW sports sedan for $40,750.88 from an authorized BMW dealer in Birmingham, Alabama. After driving the car for approximately nine months, and without noticing any flaws in its appearance, Dr. Gore took the car to "Slick Finish," an independent detailer, to make it look " 'snazzier than it normally would appear.' " 646 So. 2d 619, 621 (Ala. 1994). Mr. Slick, the proprietor, detected evidence that the car had been repainted. Convinced that he had been cheated, Dr. Gore brought suit against petitioner BMW of North America (BMW), the American distributor of BMW automobiles. Dr. Gore alleged ... that the failure to disclose that the car had been repainted constituted suppression of a material fact. ...

To prove his actual damages of $4,000, he relied on the testimony of a former BMW dealer, who estimated that the value of a repainted BMW was approximately 10 percent less than the value of a new car that had not been damaged and repaired. To support his claim for punitive damages, Dr. Gore introduced evidence that since 1983 BMW had sold 983 refinished cars as new, including 14 in Alabama, without disclosing that the cars had been repainted before sale at a cost of more than $300 per vehicle. Using the actual damage estimate of $4,000 per vehicle, Dr. Gore argued that a punitive award of $4 million would provide an appropriate penalty for selling approximately 1,000 cars for more than they were worth.

In defense of its disclosure policy, BMW argued that it was under no obligation to disclose repairs of minor damage to new cars and that Dr. Gore's car was as good as a car with the original factory finish. It disputed Dr. Gore's assertion that *v. Gore*, the U.S. Supreme Court vacated (set aside) a $2 million punitive damage award in a case with only a $4,000 compensatory damage award. A doctor had sued automobile manufacturer BMW after discovering that his vehicle had been repainted.

In 2003, the U.S. Supreme Court struck down an even larger punitive damage award in *State Farm Mutual Auto Ins. Co. v.*

---

the value of the car was impaired by the repainting and argued that this good faith belief made a punitive award inappropriate. . . .

The jury returned a verdict finding BMW liable for compensatory damages of $4,000. In addition, the jury assessed $4 million in punitive damages, based on a determination that the nondisclosure policy constituted "gross, oppressive or malicious" fraud. . . .

The Alabama Supreme Court did, however, rule in BMW's favor on one critical point: The court found that the jury improperly computed the amount of punitive damages. . . . Having found the verdict tainted, the court held that "a constitutionally reasonable punitive damages award in this case is $2,000,000." . . .

In our federal system, States necessarily have considerable flexibility in determining the level of punitive damages that they will allow in different classes of cases and in any particular case. Most States that authorize exemplary damages afford the jury similar latitude, requiring only that the damages awarded be reasonably necessary to vindicate the State's legitimate interests in punishment and deterrence. . . . Only when an award can fairly be categorized as "grossly excessive" in relation to these interests does it enter the zone of arbitrariness that violates the Due Process Clause of the Fourteenth Amendment. . . .

Elementary notions of fairness enshrined in our constitutional jurisprudence dictate that a person receive fair notice not only of the conduct that will subject him to punishment but also of the severity of the penalty that a State may impose. Three guideposts, each of which indicates that BMW did not receive adequate notice of the magnitude of the sanction that Alabama might impose for adhering to the nondisclosure policy adopted in 1983, lead us to the conclusion that the $2 million award against BMW is grossly excessive: the degree of reprehensibility of the nondisclosure; the disparity between the harm or potential harm suffered by Dr. Gore and his punitive damages award; and the difference between this remedy and the civil penalties authorized or imposed in comparable cases. . . .

Campbell.[10] In that case, the State Farm insurance company refused to settle a claim issued by a third party on behalf of an insured person. The insured person, Chris Campbell, was sued for his role in an automobile accident. The other parties in the automobile accident agreed to settle the case for $50,000, but State Farm refused to settle, assuring Campbell that he would prevail at trial. Instead, the jury imposed liability on Campbell in the amount of $185,000. When Campbell sued State Farm, the

FROM THE BENCH

Phillip Morris U.S.A. v. Williams (2007)

In our view, the Constitution's Due Process Clause forbids a State to use a punitive damages award to punish a defendant for injury that it inflicts upon nonparties or those whom they directly represent, i.e., injury that it inflicts upon those who are, essentially, strangers to the litigation. For one thing, the Due Process Clause prohibits a State from punishing an individual without first providing that individual with "an opportunity to present every available defense." ... Yet a defendant threatened with punishment for injuring a nonparty victim has no opportunity to defend against the charge, by showing, for example in a case such as this, that the other victim was not entitled to damages because he or she knew that smoking was dangerous or did not rely upon the defendant's statements to the contrary.

For another, to permit punishment for injuring a nonparty victim would add a near standardless dimension to the punitive damages equation. How many such victims are there? How seriously were they injured? Under what circumstances did injury occur? The trial will not likely answer such questions as to nonparty victims. The jury will be left to speculate. And the fundamental due process concerns to which our punitive damages cases refer—risks of arbitrariness, uncertainty, and lack of notice—will be magnified....

Finally, we can find no authority supporting the use of punitive damages awards for the purpose of punishing a defendant for harming others. We have said that it may be appropriate to consider the reasonableness of a punitive damages award in light of the potential harm the defendant's conduct could have caused. But we have made clear that the potential harm at issue was harm potentially caused the plaintiff.

jury awarded $1 million in compensatory damages, along with a whopping $145 million in punitive damages.

"A defendant should be punished for the conduct that harmed the plaintiff, not for being an unsavory individual or business," Justice Anthony Kennedy wrote for the U.S. Supreme Court. "Our jurisprudence and the principles it has now established demonstrate, however, that, in practice, few awards exceeding a single-digit ratio between punitive and compensatory damages, to a significant degree, will satisfy due process."[11] In other words, the Court said that it is rare for a ratio of punitive damages to compensatory damages to exceed 10 to 1 and still be constitutional. In the *Campbell* case, the ratio of punitive damages to compensatory damages was 145 to 1 and, therefore, too excessive, according to the Supreme Court.

The *Campbell* case has already had an effect on tobacco liability cases. For instance, on October 6, 2003, the U.S. Supreme Court struck down a punitive damage award against tobacco giant Philip Morris in the case of *Philip Morris U.S.A., Inc., v. Williams.*[12] In the *Williams* case, an Oregon jury had awarded $79.5 million in punitive damages against Philip Morris on behalf of Mayola Williams, the widow of former smoker Jesse Williams. After the Oregon Supreme Court again upheld the astronomical punitive damage award, the case reached the U.S. Supreme Court.

The Court rejected the punitive damage award, calling it "excessive" and "unconstitutional" under the due process clause. The Court pointed out that the jury had been allowed to assess punitive damages to punish a tobacco company for conduct allegedly committed against nonparties—persons other than the plaintiff.[13]

Traditionally, plaintiffs could not recover damages in a civil court suit if they assumed the risk when they undertook a certain activity. Some observers believe that juries forget or ignore the doctrine of assumption of risk. Political commentator Walter Williams writes:

As a result of the successful lawsuits against tobacco companies, assumption-of-risk doctrine is a skeleton of its past. For decades, under our traditional tort regime, if a plaintiff knows the risks of smoking, yet still smokes and contracts a tobacco-related illness, he had no claim against the tobacco manufacturer. That's all changed.[14]

Lawsuits against Big Tobacco create a slippery slope.

The suits against tobacco companies have created a dangerous precedent. Now, similar lawsuits have been filed against companies selling other harmful products, such as fatty fast foods. Already, several lawsuits have been filed against a number of fast-food restaurants, including McDonald's, Wendy's, Burger King, and Kentucky Fried Chicken. In one suit, a 57-year-old man sued various fast-food restaurants, claiming that the restaurants had failed to warn him that a steady diet of fast food would lead to health problems, such as heart disease and diabetes.[15]

Summary

Personal responsibility should guide the legal system's evaluation of suits against Big Tobacco. Even if the conduct of the tobacco giants was far less than admirable, the companies did not force people to smoke. Individuals have the freedom to choose. By imposing damages on tobacco companies, juries are punishing companies for the unfortunate personal decisions of individuals.

Advertising Restrictions Against Tobacco Products Help Protect Children and Are Constitutional

H onus Wagner, a professional baseball player at the turn of the twentieth century, is rightfully remembered for his incredible hitting and skillful base running. He may be better known today, however, for his stance against smoking.

In the early twentieth century, smoking was common and tobacco was advertised widely with limited restrictions. In fact, one common way to advertise tobacco was to give out baseball cards along with cigarettes and chewing tobacco. Like many ball-players of the time, Wagner, a Pittsburgh Pirates shortstop, had his baseball card distributed with tobacco products. Wagner was himself a nonsmoker and strongly objected to this placement of baseball cards. He believed that advertising tobacco products in a market geared toward children set a bad example for young people. In 1909, Wagner succeeded in getting his baseball card recalled. Interestingly, in the years since, the controversial card has become one of the most valuable of all time.

Commercial speech is not entitled to as much protection as other forms of speech.

Tobacco advertising is a form of commercial speech protected by the First Amendment. However, the U.S. Supreme Court has declared that commercial speech is not entitled to as much protection as political and other forms of noncommercial speech. The court has said that commercial speech receives less

FROM THE BENCH

Virginia State Board of Pharmacy v. Virginia Citizens Consumer Council, Inc., 425 U.S. 748 (1976)

The plaintiff-appellees in this case attack, as violative of the First and Fourteenth Amendments, [note 1] that portion of §54–524.35 of Va. Code Ann. (1974), which provides that a pharmacist licensed in Virginia is guilty of unprofessional [750] conduct if he "(3) publishes, advertises or promotes, directly or indirectly, in any manner whatsoever, any amount, price, fee, premium, discount, rebate or credit terms ... for any drugs which may be dispensed only by prescription." The three-judge District Court declared the quoted portion of the statute "void and of no effect," Jurisdictional Statement, App. 1, and enjoined the defendant-appellants, the Virginia State Board of Pharmacy and the individual members of that Board, from enforcing it. 373 F. Supp. 683 (ED Va. 1974)....

Since the challenged restraint is one that peculiarly concerns the licensed pharmacist in Virginia, we begin with a description of that profession as it exists under Virginia law.

The regulatory body is the appellant Virginia State Board of Pharmacy. The Board is broadly charged by statute with various responsibilities, including the "maintenance of the quality, quantity, integrity, safety and efficacy of drugs or devices distributed, dispensed or administered."...

protection "commensurate with its subordinate position in the scale of First Amendment values."[1] The court has recognized that there exists a "common-sense distinction between speech proposing a commercial transaction, which occurs in an area traditionally subject to government regulation, and other varieties of speech."[2]

The U.S. Supreme Court extended a measure of First Amendment protection to commercial speech in 1976 in *Virginia State Board of Pharmacy v. Virginia Citizens Consumer Council, Inc.* But even then, the justices still ruled that commercial speech was not

---

Inasmuch as only a licensed pharmacist may dispense prescription drugs in Virginia, advertising or other affirmative dissemination of prescription drug price information is effectively forbidden in the State....

The question first arises whether, even assuming that First Amendment protection attaches to the flow of drug price information, it is a protection enjoyed by the appellees as recipients of the information, and not solely, if at all, by the advertisers themselves who seek to disseminate that information....

The appellants contend that the advertisement of prescription drug prices is outside the protection of the First Amendment because it is "commercial speech."... [T]he Court has never denied protection on the ground that the speech in issue was "commercial speech."...

If there is a kind of commercial speech that lacks all First Amendment protection, therefore, it must be distinguished by its content....

Untruthful speech, commercial or otherwise, has never been protected for its own sake. Obviously, much commercial speech is not provably false, or even wholly false, but only deceptive or misleading. We foresee no obstacle to a State's dealing effectively with this problem. The First Amendment, as we construe it today, does not prohibit the State from insuring that the stream of commercial information flow cleanly as well as freely....

What is at issue is whether a State may completely suppress the dissemination of concededly truthful information about entirely lawful activity, fearful of that information's effect upon its disseminators and its recipients. Reserving other questions, we conclude that the answer to this one is in the negative.

entitled to full protection. The Court reasoned that commercial speech could be regulated more than political speech because it was "more easily verifiable" and "more durable."[3] The Court reasoned that the truthfulness about a price advertisement (commercial speech) could be determined more easily than a news report or political opinion. The Court also noted that commercial speech was less subject to being shut down, due to its role in ensuring commercial profit.

In *Virginia Pharmacy*, the Court also emphasized that deceptive, untruthful, and misleading commercial speech was entitled to no First Amendment protection. Since tobacco companies often engage in deceptive and misleading advertising, regulations on tobacco advertising do not violate freedom of speech.

A few years after the *Virginia Pharmacy* case, the U.S. Supreme Court established a balancing test that provided less constitutional protection for commercial speech than under *Virginia Pharmacy*. In *Central Hudson Gas & Electric Corp. v. Public Service Commission of N.Y.*, the Court ruled that restrictions on commercial speech must meet a less burdensome standard:

1. The speech must concern lawful activity and not be misleading.
2. The asserted governmental interest must be substantial.
3. The regulation must directly and materially advance the governmental interest.
4. The regulation must be no more extensive than necessary to further the governmental interest.[4]

When applying the *Central Hudson* test to tobacco ad regulations, many regulations survive judicial review. First, it is highly possible that many tobacco ads are misleading and deceptive. Second, the government surely has a substantial, if not compelling, interest in protecting minors from underage smoking. The question becomes whether the regulations directly advance the governmental interests and whether they are too broad.

The electronic ban on cigarette advertising is necessary.

The federal courts have upheld federal bans on radio and television advertisements of cigarettes. Section 6 of the Public Health Cigarette Smoking Act of 1969 provided: "It shall be unlawful to advertise cigarettes on any medium of electronic communication subject to the jurisdiction of the Federal Communications Commission."

Several corporations operating radio stations challenged the law on First Amendment free speech grounds and Fifth Amendment due process grounds. They argued that the ban violated the First Amendment because it prevented them from communicating about their products on an important medium. They claimed that the ban violated their Fifth Amendment rights because the classification between the broadcast medium and the print medium with regard to cigarettes was subjective and irrational. Due process requires that legislation have a rational basis and not be subjectively decided.

In *Capital Broadcasting Co. v. Mitchell*, a panel of three federal judges ruled 2 to 1 that the ban was constitutional. The majority rejected the First Amendment argument, noting that the corporations "have lost no right to speak—only an ability to collect revenue from others for broadcasting their commercial messages." The court ruled that the radio stations could air their own point of view about the smoking controversy. The majority also rejected the Fifth Amendment argument, finding there was a rational basis to treat the broadcast medium differently from the print medium. "Substantial evidence showed that the most persuasive advertising was being conducted on radio and television, and that these broadcasts were particularly effective in reaching a very large audience of young people," the majority wrote.[5]

The tobacco companies gave up many of their free speech rights in the Master Settlement Agreement.

On November 23, 1998, officials from 46 states, the District of Columbia, Puerto Rico, the U.S. Virgin Islands, and other U.S. territories made an agreement with the five largest tobacco manufacturers: Brown & Williamson, Lorillard Tobacco, Philip Morris, R.J. Reynolds, and Liggett & Myers. The result was the historic Master Settlement Agreement, which put major restrictions on tobacco advertising freedoms. Its aim was to reduce children's exposure to this advertising.

Four states—Florida, Minnesota, Mississippi, and Texas—had already settled with the tobacco companies for $40 billion. As part of the agreement, the companies agreed to pay more than $200 billion to the states for the next 25 years. In addition, the tobacco companies agreed to a whole host of advertising restrictions. Many of these restrictions involve advertising in places likely to be frequented by children. They include banning cartoon characters in tobacco ads, such as Joe Camel; banning outdoor tobacco advertising; banning the use of tobacco brand names at stadiums and arenas; banning distribution and sale of non-tobacco merchandise with brand-name logos (such as caps and T-shirts); and banning cigarette brands from being named after recognized non-tobacco brand names or trade names, recognized sports teams, entertainment groups, or celebrities. The agreement also calls for the removal of all tobacco billboards.

Tobacco companies have targeted children, even after the Master Settlement Agreement.

Much of the energy behind the Master Settlement Agreement was from a desire to prevent tobacco companies from advertising in venues popular among young people. Cigarette companies have repeatedly aimed their advertising at specific groups, including minorities and children. "But it's children that the tobacco companies' advertising affects most of all," comedian

Commercial expression has some protections under the First Amendment. When tobacco companies used images such as Joe Camel to advertise their products, however, it was determined that they were deliberately targeting children, which is prohibited. Here, an advertisement featuring Joe Camel in New York's Times Square is painted over in 1997 as a result of court decisions barring companies from using the character.

Steve Allen wrote in his book, *The Passionate Nonsmoker's Bill of Rights.*[6]

For years, the cartoon character "Joe Camel" and the cowboy figure "The Marlboro Man" appeared in advertisements in ways that gave cigarettes a positive image. The Joe Camel character was popular and well known among teenagers. One study by the *Journal of the American Medical Association* showed that 93 percent of high school students knew which cigarette brand was promoted by Joe Camel, compared with 58 percent of adults. In the same findings, 43 percent of the students thought Joe Camel was "cool," compared with 26 percent of adults.[7]

The government has a substantial, even compelling, interest in preventing minors from smoking. The government must have broad powers to reduce youth smoking, which is illegal. Unfortunately, tobacco companies have long been engaged in a pattern of targeting young people in an effort to attract new smokers. Plaintiffs in one case against the companies produced an internal memo from a tobacco executive stating: "[T]here is certainly nothing immoral or unethical about our Company attempting

FROM THE BENCH

Capital Broadcasting Co. v. Mitchell, 333 F.Supp. 582, 586 (D.D.C. 1971)

Substantial evidence showed that the most persuasive advertising was being conducted on radio and television, and that these broadcasts were particularly effective in reaching a very large audience of young people.

Thus, Congress knew of the close relationship between cigarette commercials broadcast on the electronic media and their potential influence on young people, and was no doubt aware that the younger the individual, the greater the reliance on the broadcast message rather than the written word.

A pre-school or early elementary school age child can hear and understand a radio commercial or see, hear and understand a television commercial, while at the same time be substantially unaffected by an advertisement printed in a newspaper, magazine or appearing on a billboard.

to attract [underage] smokers to our products." The executive also urged the company to develop new products to influence "pre-smokers to try smoking, learn to smoke, and become confirmed smokers."[8]

U.S. Senator Edward Kennedy, a Democrat from Massachusetts, writes that the tobacco companies continue to market aggressively to children:

> Contrary to industry claims, the major tobacco companies have not abandoned their aggressive marketing strategy aimed at children. The Master Settlement Agreement (MSA) entered into between the major tobacco companies and 46 states in 1998 contained an industry promise not to take any action, directly or indirectly, to target youth. Within months of making that commitment, the industry massively increased the amount it spent on marketing. . . . Much of the spending increase has been on marketing that is known to appeal to youths. A March 2002 survey found that while only 27 percent of adults had seen tobacco advertisements in the preceding two weeks, 64 percent of teenagers recalled seeing tobacco ads during that period. The industry is still promoting cigarettes in the ways most likely to reach children.[9]

The American Heart Association, however, points to studies showing that tobacco companies increased their advertising in magazines with a large youth readership *after* the signing of the Master Settlement Agreement. In California, the state attorney general sued tobacco giant R.J. Reynolds for violating the agreement by placing ads in magazines with many young readers, including *Sports Illustrated, Spin,* and *Hot Rod* magazines. A trial judge agreed and fined R.J. Reynolds $20 million. The judge ordered the tobacco corporation to "reduce youth exposure" to cigarette ads.

Still, a 2001 study reported in the *New England Journal of Medicine* concluded that the Master Settlement Agreement has had little, if any, effect on youth exposure to cigarette ads.[10] The

Department of Health and Human Services estimates that the vast majority of smokers, up to 90 percent, begin to smoke when they are 20 years of age or younger.[11]

Tobacco companies have targeted minority communities.

The Surgeon General has reported that the tobacco industry has engaged in a pattern of targeting certain minority communities:

- Studies have found a higher density of tobacco billboards in racial/ethnic minority communities. For example, a 1993 study in San Diego, California, found that the highest proportion of tobacco billboards were posted in Asian-American communities and the lowest proportion were in white communities.

- The tobacco industry commonly uses cultural symbols and designs to target racial/ethnic populations. American Spirit cigarettes were promoted as "natural" cigarettes; the package featured an American Indian smoking a pipe. In addition, certain tobacco product advertisements have used visual images, such as American Indian warriors, to target their products.

- A one-year study found that three major African-American publications—*Ebony*, *Jet*, and *Essence*—received proportionately higher profits from cigarette advertisements than did other magazines.[12]

Law professor Vernellia R. Randall writes:

The tobacco industry specifically targeted the African-American community with their product. It disproportionately flooded the African-American community with advertisement and cigarettes. It promoted a more addicting drug in the African-American community. As a result, more African-American adults smoke, are more addicted, and have greater illness due to smoking.[13]

Tobacco companies have also developed specially named brands targeting African Americans, such as Uptown Kool. "To say that the black community has been overrun with tobacco advertising is an understatement," Professor Randall writes. "The size and number of billboards in minority communities have created an intrusive and persistent form of advertising. There is absolutely no way to avoid it."[14]

Several studies have again shown that many minority communities are deluged with billboards for tobacco and alcohol products. The Centers for Disease Control and Prevention report that tobacco billboards appear in minority neighborhoods at quadruple or quintuple the rate they do in other neighborhoods. Congress continues to recognize the problem of targeted advertising by tobacco companies toward minorities. Among the findings of the Secondhand Smoke Education and Outreach Act of 2007 is the following: "Racial and ethnic minorities are disproportionately targeted with advertising campaigns for tobacco products."[15]

Summary

Restrictions on tobacco advertising are necessary in light of the industry's continued and relentless marketing campaigns. Study after study has established that tobacco companies have targeted their marketing to minorities and especially children. This is the case despite the fact that several tobacco companies have agreed to self-imposed restrictions on advertising. Even after the Master Settlement Agreement, evidence suggests that tobacco companies are still targeting new smokers who are underage. Recent lawsuits in Arizona, California, and elsewhere establish that various tobacco companies are not adhering to the agreement. The distinction between commercial and non-commercial speech has stood since the modern commercial speech doctrine was first defined in the mid 1970s with the *Virginia Pharmacy* case. Even though the U.S. Supreme Court has given more protection to commercial speech in recent years, the Court still recognizes that government has more control over commercial speech than noncommercial speech.

Tobacco Advertising Is a Form of Protected Speech

For decades, the name Winston-Salem was closely linked with the National Association for Stock Car Auto Racing, or NASCAR. Winston-Salem is the North Carolina town that is home to the R.J. Reynolds Tobacco Company. The tobacco giant sponsored NASCAR's famous Winston Racing Series for 26 years, presenting winning drivers with regional and national prizes that totaled some $1.4 million each year.

The long-term relationship between tobacco and racing came to a dramatic end in 1999. In response to the ever-growing controversy over smoking, and particularly the influence of tobacco advertisements on young people, R.J. Reynolds decided to withdraw its sponsorship of the Winston Racing Series. Part of the company's reason for the decision was the fact that in some places, NASCAR drivers are only 16 to 17 years old (under the legal age for using tobacco products). These drivers would therefore be among the age group to which cigarette companies are not permitted to advertise, according to the Master Settlement Agreement. Many racing fans were upset over the decision—fearing NASCAR would suffer financial setbacks—and they decried the end of a tradition.

Advertising, like R.J. Reynolds's former sponsorship of NASCAR, remains an important part of U.S. consumer culture.

FROM THE BENCH

Virginia State Board of Pharmacy v. Virginia Citizens Consumer Council, Inc., 425 U.S. 748,765 (1976)

Generalizing, society also may have a strong interest in the free flow of commercial information. Even an individual advertisement, though entirely "commercial," may be of general public interest.... Obviously, not all commercial messages contain the same or even a very great public interest element. There are few to which such an element, however, could not be added. Our pharmacist, for example, could cast himself as a commentator on store-to-store disparities in drug prices, giving his own and those of a competitor as proof. We see little point in requiring him to do so, and little difference if he does not.

Moreover, there is another consideration that suggests that no line between publicly "interesting" or "important" commercial advertising and the opposite kind could ever be drawn. Advertising, however tasteless and excessive it sometimes may seem, is nonetheless dissemination of information as to who is producing and selling what product, for what reason, and at what price. So long as we preserve a predominantly free enterprise economy the allocation of our resources in large measure will be made through numerous private economic decisions. It is a matter of public interest that those decisions, in the aggregate, be intelligent and well informed. To this end, the free flow of commercial information is indispensable. And if it is indispensable to the proper allocation of resources in a free enterprise system, it is also indispensable to the formation of intelligent opinions as to how that system ought to be regulated or altered. Therefore, even if the First Amendment were thought to be primarily an instrument to enlighten public decisionmaking in a democracy, we could not say that the free flow of information does not serve that goal.

The First Amendment provides a substantial degree of protection for the advertising of legal products. Unpopular as it may be, tobacco is a legal product for adults. For many years, advertising received no First Amendment protection. In the mid 1970s, however, the U.S. Supreme Court recognized that a consumer's interest in the free flow of commercial information was important enough to merit protection.

In its 1976 decision *Virginia State Board of Pharmacy v. Virginia Citizens Consumer Council, Inc.*, the Supreme Court created the commercial speech doctrine and explicitly ruled that advertising was entitled to First Amendment protection.[1] The Court recognized that the public had the right to receive information and ideas. It also determined that individuals have the right to receive the free flow of commercial information.

Even before the Supreme Court explicitly protected commercial speech under the umbrella of the First Amendment, some judges recognized that suppression of information about the smoking controversy violated freedom of speech. In the *Capital Broadcasting Co. v. Mitchell* case discussed in the previous chapter, Judge Skelly Wright dissented from the panel majority. "It would be difficult to argue that there are many who mourn for the Marlboro Man or miss the ungrammatical Winston jingles," he wrote. "Moreover, overwhelming scientific evidence makes plain that the Salem girl was in fact a seductive merchant of death—that the real 'Marlboro Country' is the graveyard. But the First Amendment does not protect only speech that is healthy or harmless."[2] Wright reasoned that the theory behind the First Amendment is based on the belief that people will make the right choice if they are presented with all points of views on controversial topics.[3]

Commercial speech deserves greater protection.

In the mid 1990s, the U.S. Supreme Court granted commercial speech even more protection, particularly in cases involving alcohol, gambling, and tobacco products. In *Rubin v. Coors*

Brewing Company, the Court unanimously struck down a regulation of the Federal Alcohol Administration Act prohibiting the display of alcoholic content on beer labels.[4] The next year, in *44 Liquormart, Inc. v. Rhode Island*, the Supreme Court struck down two Rhode Island laws that prohibited advertising the retail prices of alcoholic beverages. The state argued that the ban was necessary to reduce alcohol consumption.[5] The Court ruled that the state's ban violated the First Amendment. In a concurring opinion, Justice Clarence Thomas went so far as to call for the abandonment of the distinction between commercial and noncommercial speech: "I do not see a philosophical or historical basis for asserting that commercial speech is of lower value than noncommercial speech. Indeed, some historical materials suggest to the contrary."[6] These decisions set the stage for the Court's decision in a tobacco advertisement case.

The *Lorillard* decision upholds some commercial speech rights in regard to tobacco.

In *Lorillard Tobacco Co. v. Reilly*, the Supreme Court examined the constitutionality of several parts of a Massachusetts law designed to limit the advertising of tobacco products in the state. The attorney for the state argued that the state law was necessary to "close holes" in the Master Settlement Agreement signed by 46 states and five major tobacco manufacturers.

The law prohibited outdoor advertising and "point-of-sale" advertising of tobacco products in the state. It applied to cigarettes, cigars, and smokeless tobacco. It defined outdoor advertising as follows:

> Outdoor advertising, including advertising in enclosed stadiums and advertising from within a retail establishment that is directed toward or visible from the outside of the establishment, in any location that is within a 1,000-foot [about 300-meter] radius of any public playground, playground area in a public park, elementary school, or secondary school.[7]

It also defined point-of-sale advertising as

> advertising of cigarettes or smokeless tobacco products any
> portion of which is placed lower than 5 feet from the floor of
> any retail establishment which is located within a 1,000-foot
> radius of any public playground, playground area in a public
> park, elementary school, or secondary school, and which is
> not an adult-only retail establishment.[8]

The Supreme Court ruled that a federal law known as the Federal Cigarette Labeling and Advertising Act (FCLAA) overruled Massachusetts's advertising restrictions as applied to cigarettes. One provision of the FCLAA provided that "no requirement or prohibition based on smoking and health shall be imposed under State law with respect to the advertising or promotion of any cigarettes the packages of which are labeled in conformity with the provisions of this chapter."[9]

The tobacco companies argued that this provision of federal law means that the Massachusetts law regulating cigarette advertising was unconstitutional because it infringed on an area of exclusive federal domain. The state argued that the federal law did not preempt its law because the federal law only preempted state laws dealing with the content of tobacco advertising. Because its law was purely a restriction based on where advertising could be placed—not its content—the state argued that FCLAA had no effect upon it.

The Supreme Court, however, disagreed with the state and found preemption: "a distinction between state regulation of the location as opposed to the content of cigarette advertising has no foundation in the text of the preemption provision."[10]

The Court then examined whether the outdoor advertising and point-of-sale bans on cigars and smokeless tobacco products violated the First Amendment. The Court determined that the state attorney general had a serious interest in protecting minors from tobacco products. But it decided that the 1,000-foot

FROM THE BENCH

Lorillard Tobacco Co. v. Reilly, 533 U.S. 525 (2001).

Justice O'Connor delivered the opinion of the Court.

In January 1999, the Attorney General of Massachusetts promulgated comprehensive regulations governing the advertising and sale of cigarettes, smokeless tobacco, and cigars. Petitioners, a group of cigarette, smokeless tobacco, and cigar manufacturers and retailers, filed suit in Federal District Court claiming that the regulations violate federal law and the United States Constitution. The first question presented for our review is whether certain cigarette advertising regulations are preempted by the Federal Cigarette Labeling and Advertising Act (FCLAA). The second question presented is whether certain regulations governing the advertising and sale of tobacco products violate the First Amendment....

For over 25 years, the Court has recognized that commercial speech does not fall outside the purview of the First Amendment. Instead, the Court has afforded commercial speech a measure of First Amendment protection 'commensurate' with its position in relation to other constitutionally guaranteed expression. In recognition of the "distinction between speech proposing a commercial transaction, which occurs in an area traditionally subject to government regulation, and other varieties of speech," we developed a framework for analyzing regulations of commercial speech that is "substantially similar" to the test for time, place, and manner restrictions. The analysis contains four elements: "At the outset, we must determine whether the expression is protected by the First Amendment. For commercial speech to come within that provision, it at least must concern lawful activity and not be misleading. Next, we ask whether the asserted governmental interest is substantial. If both inquiries yield positive answers, we must determine whether the regulation directly advances the governmental interest asserted, and whether it is not more extensive than is necessary to serve that interest." ...

The Attorney General has assumed for purposes of summary judgment that petitioners' speech is entitled to First Amendment protection. With respect to the second step, none of the petitioners contests the importance of the State's interest in preventing the use of tobacco products by minors....

The Attorney General relies in part on evidence gathered by the Food and Drug Administration (FDA) in its attempt to regulate the advertising of cigarettes and smokeless tobacco. The FDA promulgated the advertising regulations after finding that the period prior to adulthood is when an overwhelming majority of Americans first decide to use tobacco products, and that advertising plays a crucial role in that decision. We later held that the FDA lacks statutory authority to regulate tobacco products. Nevertheless, the Attorney General relies on the FDA's proceedings and other studies to support his decision that advertising affects demand for tobacco products....

The State's interest in preventing underage tobacco use is substantial, and even compelling, but it is no less true that the sale and use of tobacco products by adults is a legal activity. We must consider that tobacco retailers and manufacturers have an interest in conveying truthful information about their products to adults, and adults have a corresponding interest in receiving truthful information about tobacco products.... As the State protects children from tobacco advertisements, tobacco manufacturers and retailers and their adult consumers still have a protected interest in communication.

In some instances, Massachusetts' outdoor advertising regulations would impose particularly onerous burdens on speech.... If some retailers have relatively small advertising budgets, and use few avenues of communication, then the Attorney General's outdoor advertising regulations potentially place a greater, not lesser, burden on those retailers' speech....

We conclude that the Attorney General has failed to show that the outdoor advertising regulations for smokeless tobacco and cigars are not more extensive than necessary to advance the State's substantial interest in preventing underage tobacco use....

In this case, Congress enacted a comprehensive scheme to address cigarette smoking and health in advertising and preempted state regulation of cigarette advertising that attempts to address that same concern, even with respect to youth. The First Amendment also constrains state efforts to limit advertising of tobacco products, because so long as the sale and use of tobacco is lawful for adults, the tobacco industry has a protected interest in communicating information about its products and adult customers have an interest in receiving that information.

To the extent that federal law and the First Amendment do not prohibit state action, States and localities remain free to combat the problem of underage tobacco use by appropriate means.

restriction on outdoor advertising was simply too broad. "In some geographical areas, these regulations would constitute nearly a complete ban on the communication of truthful information about smokeless tobacco and cigars to adult consumers," the Court wrote.[11]

The justices pointed out the fact that the regulations would restrict the free speech rights of adults, too. Even though the state has a substantial interest in protecting minors from tobacco usage, tobacco manufacturers and adult consumers have a First Amendment right to provide and receive information about lawful products. "The State's interest in preventing underage tobacco use is substantial, and even compelling, but it is by no means less true that the sale and use of tobacco products by adults is a legal activity," the Court wrote. Citing a case about the restriction of indecent speech on the Internet, the Court emphasized that the government cannot use the protection of minors as a means to suppress the free speech rights of adults.[12]

FROM THE BENCH

Lorillard Tobacco Co. v. Reilly, 533 U.S. 525 (2001).

Justice Clarence Thomas's concurring opinion:

No legislature has ever sought to restrict speech about an activity it regarded as harmless and inoffensive. Calls for limits on expression always are made when the specter of some threatened harm is looming. The identity of the harm may vary. People will be inspired by totalitarian dogmas and subvert the Republic. They will be inflamed by racial demagoguery and embrace hatred and bigotry. Or they will be enticed by cigarette advertisements and choose to smoke, risking disease. It is therefore no answer for the State to say that the makers of cigarettes are doing harm: perhaps they are. But in that respect they are no different from the purveyors of other harmful products, or the advocates of harmful ideas. When the State seeks to silence them, they are all entitled to the protection of the First Amendment.

The Court declared that the 1,000-foot ban on outdoor advertising was particularly onerous because the law's definition of outdoor advertising included advertising in stores if the ad could be seen from outside the store. In addition to this, the court struck down the point-of-sale provision prohibiting advertising fewer than five feet from the floor of retail advertisements. The majority determined that this restriction did not advance the state's goals in protecting minors. "Not all children are less than 5 feet tall, and those who are certainly have the ability to look up and take in their surroundings."[13]

Justice Clarence Thomas wrote separately to emphasize his oft-stated view that commercial speech, including tobacco advertising, should not receive second-class status in First Amendment jurisprudence:

> The state of Massachusetts could have used other means to try to prevent underage tobacco smoking. These means would not have violated the First Amendment. The state could have more vigorously enforced its existing laws prohibiting the sale of tobacco to minors. The state could have financed its own anti-tobacco messages or the state could have initiated youth programs designed to warn about the dangers of smoking.[14]

Even the justices who dissented on the preemption issue were troubled by the outdoor advertising regulations. In his dissent, justice John Paul Stevens said that he would favor sending the case down to the lower court for the development of further evidence on the breadth of the regulation.

One legal commentator has written that the *Lorillard* decision:

> effectively places advertising on the same constitutional level as advertising for other lawful goods and services under the First Amendment, and creates a strong likelihood that laws restricting the flow of protected commercial speech in order to manipulate consumer behavior are likely to be struck down

as unconstitutional, despite a compelling regulatory interest, such as protecting the health of minors.[15]

Many states ignore the fact that federal law preempts state laws on the regulation of tobacco advertising. In their excessive zeal to regulate tobacco advertising, the states intrude upon the reach of the Federal Cigarette Labeling and Advertising Act of 1965. For example, the state of Washington passed a law

Excerpts from Master Settlement Agreement, 1998

WHEREAS, more than 40 States have commenced litigation asserting various claims for monetary, equitable and injunctive relief against certain tobacco product manufacturers and others as defendants, and the States that have not filed suit can potentially assert similar claims ...

WHEREAS, defendants have denied each and every one of the Settling States' allegations of unlawful conduct or wrongdoing and have asserted a number of defenses to the Settling States' claims, which defenses have been contested by the Settling States;

WHEREAS, the Settling States and the Participating Manufacturers are committed to reducing underage tobacco use by discouraging such use and by preventing Youth access to Tobacco Products ...

NOW, THEREFORE, BE IT KNOWN THAT, in consideration of the implementation of tobacco-related health measures and the payments to be made by the Participating Manufacturers, the release and discharge of all claims by the Settling States, and such other consideration as described herein, the sufficiency of which is hereby acknowledged, the Settling States and the Participating Manufacturers, acting by and through their authorized agents, memorialize and agree as follows ...

III. Permanent Relief
  (a) *Prohibition on Youth Targeting.* No Participating Manufacturer may take any action, directly or indirectly, to target Youth within any Settling State in the advertising, promotion or marketing of Tobacco Products, or take any

prohibiting the promotional "sampling" of tobacco products, even to adults. Oftentimes, tobacco companies—just like businesses of all stripes—distribute their products at a reduced price for the public to sample their product. Washington sought to ban this practice for tobacco companies, but R.J. Reynolds successfully challenged the ban in federal court. In *R.J. Reynolds Co. v. McKenna*, a federal district court ruled that federal law preempted the Washington state law. The court noted that

action the primary purpose of which is to initiate, maintain or increase the incidence of Youth smoking within any Settling State.

(b) *Ban on Use of Cartoons.* Beginning 180 days after the MSA Execution Date, no Participating Manufacturer may use or cause to be used any Cartoon in the advertising, promoting, packaging or labeling of Tobacco Products.

(c) *Limitation of Tobacco Brand Name Sponsorships.*

   (1) *Prohibited Sponsorships.* After the MSA Execution Date, no Participating Manufacturer may engage in any Brand Name Sponsorship in any State consisting of:

   (A) concerts; or

   (B) events in which the intended audience is comprised of a significant percentage of Youth; or

   (C) events in which any paid participants or contestants are Youth; or

   (D) any athletic event between opposing teams in any football, basketball, baseball, soccer or hockey league …

   (3) *Related Sponsorship Restrictions.* With respect to any Brand Name Sponsorship permitted under this subsection (c):

   (A) advertising of the Brand Name Sponsorship event shall not advertise any Tobacco Product (other than the Brand Name to identify such Brand Name Sponsorship event);

   (B) no Participating Manufacturer may refer to a Brand Name Sponsorship event or to a celebrity or other person in such an event in its advertising of a Tobacco Product.

"allowing individual states to regulate sampling could lead to diverse, nonuniform, and confusing regulations governing the promotion of cigarettes in contradiction to the express purpose of the preemption provisions of the FCLAA."[16]

The Master Settlement Agreement was unconstitutional and set a bad precedent.

In the 1998 Master Settlement Agreement, the tobacco industry voluntarily agreed to abide by a series of advertising restrictions and to pay billions of dollars in damages to the states. The restrictions on advertising in the Master Settlement Agreement are onerous. They include:

- Tobacco ads are limited to black-and-white backgrounds except for "adult-only facilities" and "adult publications."

- Tobacco companies cannot use cartoon characters, such as Joe Camel, to advertise their products.

- Tobacco companies cannot target youth in the advertising, promotion, or marketing of tobacco products.

- Tobacco companies cannot sponsor concerts or other events with significant youth audiences, including sporting events such as football games.

- Tobacco brand names cannot be advertised at stadiums and arenas.

- Tobacco outdoor advertising is banned, including billboards, signs, and placards larger than a poster.

- Tobacco companies cannot pay entertainment executives to promote tobacco products in television shows, movies, live performances, and video games.

Legal experts have noted that many of these advertising restrictions in the Master Settlement Agreement would not hold water if they were passed by a legislative body and challenged in court. "Many of the restrictions on advertising included in the settlement agreement could not be imposed legislatively because they would violate the First Amendment," says Richard Samp, chief counsel of the Washington Legal Foundation.[17]

Others point out that the Master Settlement Agreement presents other constitutional problems aside from the First Amendment. Lawyer Margaret Little writes: "The MSA is extra-constitutional legislation crafted outside of any statehouse or Congress in disregard of the structural constitutions it displaces, and it constitutes bad public policy and worse precedent."[18]

Summary

Tobacco is unquestionably a harmful product, but it is still legal in the United States. The Supreme Court has pointed out that the First Amendment provides that consumers in a free society can make their own choices and that the government cannot suppress truthful speech, even about harmful products. Under the Court's commercial speech doctrine, the government can only restrict truthful commercial speech if it shows that its regulations directly advance and further substantial governmental interests. Furthermore, the government cannot use the protection of minors as the rationale to restrict the free speech rights of adults. The basic theory behind the First Amendment is that the government cannot suppress speech, particularly truthful speech, about lawful products and issues of public importance.

Smoking Bans in the Future

More than 20 years ago, Judge Skelly Wright wrote, "cigarette smoking and the danger to health which it poses are among the most controversial and important issues before the American public today."[1] Today, the controversy over the danger of cigarette smoking has morphed into many controversies over public smoking bans, suits against Big Tobacco, and First Amendment battles. The fierce arguments sparked by the issue of smoking have not ended. If anything, they threaten to explode into even bigger debates. The lawsuits against tobacco companies continue and will not likely abate, as victims more frequently file lawsuits seeking compensation for their hardships.

The U.S. Congress continues to introduce bills regularly that address tobacco and health. In 2007, Congressman Edward Kennedy introduced a comprehensive measure called the Family Smoking Prevention and Tobacco Control Act. It contains

The trend toward banning smoking in more and more places has continued. Above, students at the University of South Maine smoke outside and at least 50 feet away from their dormitory, as required by university regulations.

numerous restrictions on tobacco advertising, including the following findings:

Tobacco advertising and marketing contribute significantly to the use of nicotine-containing tobacco products by adolescents.

Because past efforts to restrict advertising and marketing of tobacco products have failed adequately to curb tobacco use by adolescents, comprehensive restrictions on the sale, promotion, and distribution of such products are needed. . . .

The sale, distribution, marketing, advertising, and use of tobacco products are activities in and substantially affecting interstate commerce because they are sold, marketed, advertised, and distributed in interstate commerce on a nationwide basis, and have a substantial effect on the Nation's economy.[2]

The Family Smoking Prevention and Tobacco Control Act also includes mandated warnings that must be included on smokeless tobacco products.

Legislators continue to introduce bills requiring more explicit warning labels and giving the U.S. Food and Drug Administration the authority to regulate tobacco products. But not all measures in the legislature target the tobacco industry as a villain. For instance, a resolution introduced in Congress by a senator from South Carolina (a state that makes enormous profits from tobacco crops) commended the tobacco company R.J. Reynolds for its past relationship with motor sports and stock-car racing.

Not only does the tobacco issue play a prominent role in the legislature, but the courts continue to hear cases filed against the tobacco industry and cases challenging smoking bans. These cases involve issues of social and individual responsibility, expanded governmental power, tort reform, products liability, class-action lawsuits, and more.

Mandated Warnings Under Proposed Federal Legislation

It shall be unlawful for any person to manufacture, package, sell, offer to sell, distribute, or import for sale or distribution within the United States any smokeless tobacco product unless the product package bears, in accordance with the requirements of the Act, one of the following labels:

WARNING: This product can cause mouth cancer.
WARNING: This product can cause gum disease and tooth loss.
WARNING: This product is not a safe alternative to cigarettes.
WARNING: Smokeless tobacco is addictive.

Source: S. 625 Family Smoking Prevention and Tobacco Control Act

Meanwhile, tobacco companies continue to make huge sums of money and spend millions upon millions of dollars aggressively marketing their products. Current cases will determine whether the tobacco companies have violated provisions of the Master Settlement Agreement—in particular, the provisions against marketing to children. It also remains to be seen whether the tobacco giants will continue to abide by the agreement.

The issue of the dangers of secondhand smoke will keep raging as medical and scientific research continues to explore the effects of secondhand smoke. Will the movement toward limiting secondhand smoke lead to the banning of smoking in residential complexes? Will more parents lose child custody cases because of their smoking habits?

All of these questions confirm that smoking remains a hot-button issue in American society. But the issue goes beyond American society. In the past decade, numerous countries have implemented smoking bans in public places. In January 2005, Italy passed a law banning smoking in enclosed public places. In February 2006, Great Britain's Parliament approved of a similar ban on smoking in public places.[3] France, too, joined the movement and put its own public smoking ban into effect in January 2008. It is clear that controversies over the regulation of smoking have become a worldwide issue.

APPENDIX ||||| ▷

Beginning Legal Research

The goals of each book in the Point-Counterpoint series are not only to give the reader a basic introduction to a controversial issue affecting society, but also to encourage the reader to explore the issue more fully. This Appendix is meant to serve as a guide to the reader in researching the current state of the law as well as exploring some of the public policy arguments as to why existing laws should be changed or new laws are needed.

Although some sources of law can be found primarily in law libraries, legal research has become much faster and more accessible with the advent of the Internet. This Appendix discusses some of the best starting points for free access to laws and court decisions, but surfing the Web will uncover endless additional sources of information. Before you can research the law, however, you must have a basic understanding of the American legal system.

The most important source of law in the United States is the Constitution. Originally enacted in 1787, the Constitution outlines the structure of our federal government, as well as setting limits on the types of laws that the federal government and state governments can enact. Through the centuries, a number of amendments have added to or changed the Constitution, most notably the first 10 amendments, which collectively are known as the "Bill of Rights" and which guarantee important civil liberties.

Reading the plain text of the Constitution provides little information. For example, the Constitution prohibits "unreasonable searches and seizures" by the police. To understand concepts in the Constitution, it is necessary to look to the decisions of the U.S. Supreme Court, which has the ultimate authority in interpreting the meaning of the Constitution. For example, the U.S. Supreme Court's 2001 decision in *Kyllo v. United States* held that scanning the outside of a person's house using a heat sensor to determine whether the person is growing marijuana is an unreasonable search—if it is done without first getting a search warrant from a judge. Each state also has its own constitution and a supreme court that is the ultimate authority on its meaning.

Also important are the written laws, or "statutes," passed by the U.S. Congress and the individual state legislatures. As with constitutional provisions, the U.S. Supreme Court and the state supreme courts are the ultimate authorities in interpreting the meaning of federal and state laws, respectively. However, the U.S. Supreme Court might find that a state law violates the U.S. Constitution, and a state supreme court might find that a state law violates either the state or U.S. Constitution.

Not every controversy reaches either the U.S. Supreme Court or the state supreme courts, however. Therefore, the decisions of other courts are also important. Trial courts hear evidence from both sides and make a decision, while appeals courts review the decisions made by trial courts. Sometimes rulings from appeals courts are appealed further to the U.S. Supreme Court or the state supreme courts.

Lawyers and courts refer to statutes and court decisions through a formal system of citations. Use of these citations reveals which court made the decision or which legislature passed the statute, and allows one to quickly locate the statute or court case online or in a law library. For example, the Supreme Court case *Brown v. Board of Education* has the legal citation 347 U.S. 483 (1954). At a law library, this 1954 decision can be found on page 483 of volume 347 of the U.S. Reports, which are the official collection of the Supreme Court's decisions. On the following page, you will find sample of all the major kinds of legal citation.

Finding sources of legal information on the Internet is relatively simple thanks to "portal" sites such as findlaw.com and lexisone.com, which allow the user to access a variety of constitutions, statutes, court opinions, law review articles, news articles, and other useful sources of information. For example, findlaw.com offers access to all Supreme Court decisions since 1893. Other useful sources of information include gpo.gov, which contains a complete copy of the U.S. Code, and thomas.loc.gov, which offers access to bills pending before Congress, as well as recently passed laws. Of course, the Internet changes every second of every day, so it is best to do some independent searching.

Of course, many people still do their research at law libraries, some of which are open to the public. For example, some state governments and universities offer the public access to their law collections. Law librarians can be of great assistance, as even experienced attorneys need help with legal research from time to time.

Common Citation Forms

Source of Law	Sample Citation	Notes
U.S. Supreme Court	*Employment Division v. Smith*, 485 U.S. 660 (1988)	The U.S. Reports is the official record of Supreme Court decisions. There is also an unofficial Supreme Court ("S. Ct.") reporter.
U.S. Court of Appeals	*United States v. Lambert*, 695 F.2d 536 (11th Cir.1983)	Appellate cases appear in the Federal Reporter, designated by "F." The 11th Circuit has jurisdiction in Alabama, Florida, and Georgia.
U.S. District Court	*Carillon Importers, Ltd. v. Frank Pesce Group, Inc.*, 913 F.Supp. 1559 (S.D.Fla.1996)	Federal trial-level decisions are reported in the Federal Supplement ("F. Supp."). Some states have multiple federal districts; this case originated in the Southern District of Florida.
U.S. Code	Thomas Jefferson Commemoration Commission Act, 36 U.S.C., §149 (2002)	Sometimes the popular names of legislation—names with which the public may be familiar—are included with the U.S. Code citation.
State Supreme Court	*Sterling v. Cupp*, 290 Ore. 611, 614, 625 P.2d 123, 126 (1981)	The Oregon Supreme Court decision is reported in both the state's reporter and the Pacific regional reporter.
State Statute	Pennsylvania Abortion Control Act of 1982, 18 Pa. Cons. Stat. 3203-3220 (1990)	States use many different citation formats for their statutes.

Case Law and Legislation

44 Liquormart, Inc., v. Rhode Island, 517 U.S. 484 (1996)

U.S. Supreme Court rules that Rhode Island laws banning alcohol price ads are unconstitutional. This case has set a leading precedence in other commercial speech cases.

Austin v. Tennessee, 179 U.S. 343 (1900)

U.S. Supreme Court upholds a Tennessee law restricting the sale of cigarettes based on public health and safety and general police power of state.

Brashear v. Simms, 138 F.Supp.2d 693 (D. Md. 2001)

Federal district court rules against an inmate who alleges that smoking is a disability under the Americans with Disabilities Act.

Burton v. R.J. Reynolds Tobacco Company, 205 F.Supp.2d 1253 (D.Kan. 2002)

Federal district court rules that a smoker is entitled to recover punitive damages from a tobacco company for its culpable conduct.

Capital Broadcasting Company v. Mitchell, 333 F.Supp. 582 (D.D.C. 1971)

Federal court upholds a federal broadcast ban on cigarette advertisements.

Central Hudson Gas & Electric Corp. v. Public Serv. Comm'n of N.Y., 447 U.S. 557 (1980)

U.S. Supreme Court sets up a four-part test to determine the constitutionality of restrictions that impact commercial speech.

D.A.R.E., Inc. v. Toledo-Lucas County Bd. of Health, 773 N.E.2d 536 (Ohio 2002)

Ohio supreme court rules that the county health board lacked the authority to adopt clean indoor air and antismoking regulation.

Fagan v. Axelrod, 550 N.Y.S.2d 552 (N.Y 1990)

New York court upholds the state's Clean Indoor Air Law.

Flue-Cured Tobacco Cooperative Stabilization Corporation v. United States Environmental Protection Agency, 4 F.Supp.2d 435 (M.D. N.C. 1998)

Federal judge questions the validity of an EPA study on the harm of secondhand smoke.

Flue-Cured Tobacco Cooperative Stabilization Corporation v. United States Environmental Protection Agency, 313 EM 852 (4th Cir. 2002)

Federal appeals court reverses a lower-court ruling on an EPA study.

Gibbs v. Republic Tobacco, L.P., 119 F.Supp.2d 1288 (M.D. Fla. 2000)

Federal district court rules that loose-leaf tobacco is not an unreasonably dangerous product.

Goddard v. R.J. Reynolds Tobacco Company, 75 E3d 1075 (Ariz. 2003)

Arizona appeals court case deals with a tobacco company's alleged violation of the Master Settlement Agreement.

Guilbeault v. R.J. Reynolds Tobacco Company, 84 F.Supp.2d 263 (D.R.I. 2000)
Federal district court rules that the common-knowledge doctrine prevents plaintiffs' products liability claim against a tobacco company.

Helling v. McKinney, 509 U.S. 25 (1993)
U.S. Supreme Court decision deals with a prisoner's lawsuit against prison officials for failing to protect the inmate from high levels of secondhand smoke.

Huddleston v. R.J. Reynolds Tobacco Company, 66 F.Supp.2d 1370 (N.D. Ga. 1999)
Federal district court rules that Georgia state law does not recognize a claim for intentional exposure to a hazardous substance.

Liggett Group, Inc. v. Engle, 853 So.2d 434 (Fla. 2003)
Florida supreme court rules that a punitive damage award against a tobacco company is invalid in a class-action suit.

Lorillard Tobacco Co. v. Reilly, 533 U.S. 525 (2001)
U.S. Supreme Court decides on tobacco outdoor advertising, addressing both First Amendment and preemption issues.

Loyal Order of Moose Incorporated, Yarmouth Lodge #2270 v. Board of Health of Yarmouth, 790 N.E.2d 203 (2003)
State high court rules that a city smoking ban cannot be extended to a private lodge.

Nader v. Federal Aviation Administration, 440 F.2d 292 (D.C. Cir. 1971)
Federal appeals court rules against consumer advocate Ralph Nader in a suit advocating for a smoking ban on airline flights.

Philip Morris U.S.A. v. Williams, —U.S.—, 127 S.Ct. 1057 (2007)
U.S. Supreme Court rejects a large punitive damage award against a major tobacco company because the jury impermissibly considered the alleged harm caused by the company to persons other than the plaintiff or person that filed the lawsuit.

R.J. Reynolds Tobacco Co. v. McKenna, 445 F.Supp. 2d 1052 (W.D. Wash. 2006)
Federal district court rules that federal law preempts a Washington state law regulating the sampling of tobacco products for adults.

Roysdon v. R.J. Reynolds Tobacco Company, 849 F.2d 230 (6th Cir. 1988)
Federal appeals court rules that tobacco cigarettes were not defective within the meaning of Tennessee products liability law.

Shimp v. New Jersey Bell Telephone Company, 145 N.J. Super. 516, 368 A.2d 408 (1976)
New Jersey court decision holds that an employer has a duty to provide a smoke-free, safe environment for an employee sensitive to secondhand smoke.

Soliman v. Philip Morris, Inc., **311 EM 966 (9th Cir. 2002)**
Federal appeals court rules that a smoker loses on a fraudulent concealment claim against a tobacco company.

Tompkins v. R.J. Reynolds Tobacco Company, **92 F.Supp.2d 70 (N.D.N.Y 2000)**
Federal district court rules that a tobacco manufacturer is not liable on express warrant claim and had no duty to disclose.

Toole v. Brown & Williamson Tobacco Corporation, **980 F.Supp. 419 (N.D. Ala. 1997)**
Federal district court rules that tobacco cigarettes were not an unreasonably dangerous product within the meaning of Alabama's products liability law.

Virginia State Bd. of Pharmacy v. Virginia Citizens Consumer Council, Inc., **425 U.S. 748 (1976)**
U.S. Supreme Court rules on a landmark commercial speech case.

Wajda v. R.J. Reynolds Tobacco Company, **103 F.Supp.2d 29 (D.Mass. 2000)**
Federal district court rules that a tobacco company cannot be civilly liable under the RICO (Racketeer Influenced and Corrupt Organizations) Act.

Waterhouse v. R.J. Reynolds Tobacco Company, **270 F.Supp.2d 678 (D. Md. 2003)**
Federal district court bars a fraudulent concealment claim against a tobacco company. The court also rules that the plaintiffs' civil conspiracy claim can move forward.

Terms and Concepts

causation
commercial speech
comparative negligence
contributory negligence
due process
First Amendment
negligence
preemption
products liability
punitive damages
secondhand smoke
statute
tort

Introduction: The History of Tobacco and Its Regulation

1 *Lorillard Tobacco Co. v. Reilly*, 533 U.S. 525, 587 (2001), citing Amicus Brief for United States, 19.
2 Richard Kluger, *Ashes to Ashes* (New York: Alfred A. Knopf, 1996), 15.
3 *Ibid.*, 16.
4 *Austin v. Tennessee*, 179 U.S. 343 (1900).
5 *Ibid.*, 349.
6 *Ibid.*, 362.
7 Kluger, *Ashes to Ashes*, 68.
8 *Ibid.*, 109.
9 Philip J. Hilts, *Smokescreen: The Truth Behind the Tobacco Industry Coverup* (Reading, MA: Addison-Wesley Publishing Company, 1996), 1.
10 Kluger, *Ashes to Ashes*, 114.
11 *Ibid.*, 196.
12 *Ibid.*, 205.
13 *Ibid.*, 232.
14 *Ibid.*, 242.
15 *Ibid.*, 266.
16 Martin Redish, "First Amendment Theory and the Demise of the Commercial Speech Distinction: The Case of the Smoking Controversy," 24 N. Ky. L. Rev. 553, 579 (1997).
17 "Tobacco Industry Spent More Than $20 Million to Lobby Congress in 2002," Campaign for Tobacco-Free Kids, http://www.tobaccofreekids.org/Script/DisplayPressRelease.php3?Display=682.
18 *FDA v. Brown & Williamson Tobacco Corp.*, 529 U.S. 120 (2000).

Point: Smoking Bans Protect Public Health

1 Randy Hall, "Jury Finds Cigarette Companies Not Liable for Flight Attendant's Lung Cancer," *CNSNews.com*. Available online at http://www.cnsnews.com/ViewNation.asp?Page=\Nation\archive\200310\NAT20031015c.html.
2 Del. Code Ann. 16 Section 2901–2908 (2001).
3 Rosemarie Henson et al., "Clean Indoor Air: Where, Why and How," 30 J.L. Med. & Ethics 75, 77 (2002).
4 Dana Bartholomew, "Calabasas Council May Evict Smoke From Apartments," Daily News, June 21, 2007, 3.
5 Samuel J. Winokur, "Seeing Through the Smoke: The Need for National Leg- islation Banning Smoking in Bars and Restaurants," 75 *George Washington Law Review* 662, 662 (2007).
6 See S. 2005 (2007): Findings of the Secondhand Smoke Education and Outreach Act of 2007.
7 Peter Michael, "Smoking bans reduce asthma," *Sunday Mail*, January 7, 2001, 8.
8 Erik Schelzig, "Bredesen throws support behind workplace smoking ban," The Associated Press, February 9, 2007.
9 Cigarette Labeling and Advertising Act, 15 U.S.C. 1333 (1965).
10 Peter D. Jacobsen, Jeffrey Wasserman, and John R. Anderson, "Historical Overview of Tobacco Legislation and Regulation," in *Smoking: Who Has the Right?*, ed. Jeffrey A. Schaler and Magda E. Schaler, 47 (Amherst, NY: Prometheus Books, 1993).
11 EPA, "Fact Sheet: Respiratory Health Effects of Passive Smoking." Available online at http://www.epa.gov/smokefree/pubs/etsfs.html. Accessed January 25, 2008.
12 *Ibid.*
13 National Cancer Institute, "Secondhand Smoke: Questions and Answers." Available online at http://www.cancer.gov/cancertopics/factsheet/Tobacco/ETS. Accessed January 25, 2008.
14 *Shimp v. New Jersey Bell Telephone Company*, 145 N.J. Super. 516, 526, 368 A.2d 408, 413 (1976).
15 *Ibid.*, 416.
16 *Wilhelm v. CSX Transportation*, 2003 U.S. App. LEXIS 10864 (6th Cir.) (May 29, 2003).
17 *City of Tucson v. Grezaffi*, 200 Ariz. 130, 23 P3d 675 (2001).
18 49 U.S.C. Section 41706.
19 *Nader v. Federal Aviation Administrator*, 440 F.2d 292, 294–295 (D.C. Cit. 1971).
20 Carrie-Anne Tondo, "When Parents Are On a Level Playing Field, Courts Cry Foul at Smoking," 40 *Family Court Review* 238, 246 (2002).
21 David B. Ezra, "'Get Your Ashes Out of My Living Room!' Controlling Tobacco Smoke In Multi-Unit Residential Housing," 54 Rutgers Law Review 135, 139 (2001).
22 *Helling v. McKinney*, 509 U.S. 25 (1993).
23 *Ibid.*, 33.

24 *Brashear v. Simms*, 138 F.Supp.2d 693, 694 (2001).
25 Polly Curtis, "The smoking issue: THE IMPACT: Do bans help people quit?" *The Guardian*, May 14, 2007, 22.
26 Barbara Isaacs, "Study finds ban reduced smoking in Lexington," *The Lexington Herald-Leader*, December 11, 2006, A1.
27 Winokur, "Seeing Through the Smoke," 667.

Counterpoint: Smoking Bans Infringe on Smokers' Individual Rights

1 Robert W. Tracinski, "The Hazards of a Smoke-Free Environment," CNSNews.com, http://www.cnsnews.com/Commentary/Archive/200310/COM20031027d.html.
2 "Man Fired For Smoking in Home," *BBCNews.com*. Available online at http://news.bbc.co.uk/1/hi/england/1657624.stm. Accessed January 25, 2008.
3 Douglas J. Den Uyl, "Smoking, Human Liberties, and Civil Liberties," *Smoking: Who Has the Right?*, eds. Jeffrey A. Schaler and Magda E. Schaler, 267–291 (Amherst, NY: Prometheus Books, 1993).
4 Mark Edward Lender, "The New Prohibition," http://www.brownandwilliamson.com/index_sub2.cfm?Page=/BWT/Index.cfm%3FID%3D98%26Sect%3D4.
5 Sidney Zion, "Science and Secondhand Smoke: The Need for a Good Puff of Skepticism," *Skeptic* 13, November 3, 2007, 20–26, 20.
6 P. Boffetta, A. Agudo, W. Ahrens, et al., "Multicenter case-control study of exposure to environmental tobacco smoke and lung cancer in Europe," *Journal of the National Cancer Institute* 90 no. 19, (1998): 1440–1450. Abstract at http://jncicancerspectrum.oupjournals.org/cgi/content/abstract/jnci;90/19/1440?fulltext=^searchid=QID_NOT_SET.
7 Available online at http://www.rjrt.com/TI/TIHealth_Issues.asp.
8 4 F.Supp.2d 435 (M.D. N.C. 1998).
9 *Ibid.*, p. 463.
10 *Ibid.*, p. 466.
11 *Flue-Cured Tobacco Cooperative Stabilization Corporation v. United States Environmental Protection Agency*, 313 F.3d 852, 862 (4th Cir. 2002).
12 D. Dowd Muska, "A Raw Deal for Secondhand Smoke," *Nevada Journal*, August 5, 1998, http://www.npri.org/issues/issues98/I_b080598.htm.
13 *Empire State Restaurant and Tavern Association v. New York State*, complaint at p. 11, n. 52.
14 *D.A.B.E., Inc. v. Toledo-Lucas County Bd. of Health*, 773 N.E.2d 536 (Ohio 2002).
15 Jason Hardin, "Rep. Altman files bill against smoking bans," *Charleston (S.C.) Post & Courier*, June 4, 2003.
16 *Loyal Order of Moose, Incorporated, Yarmouth Lodge #2270 v. Board of Health of Yarmouth*, 790 N.E.2d 203 (2003).
17 Toby Coleman, "Power at center of court debate, Justices will decide if county smoking bans are legal," *Charleston (W.V.) Daily Mail*, October 8, 2003, 3C.
18 *Best Lock Corporation v. Review Board of the Indiana Department of Employment and Training Services*, 572 N.E.2d 520, 525 (1991).
19 Scott Wexler, "Data show indoor smoking ban has been bad for business," *The Times Union*, April 13, 2004, A8.
20 Quoted in Suzanne Bohan, "Outdoor smoking bans rile anti-tobacco leader; Pioneering crusader and others see total public prohibition as too strict," *Contra Costa Times*, January 15, 2007, F4.
21 Adrienne T. Washington, "After smokers, who will Big Brother target next?" *The Washington Times*, June 3, 2003, B02.

Point: Suits Against Big Tobacco Are Legitimate Cases Against Wealthy Defendants Selling Harmful Products

1 Catherine Heins and the Associated Press, "Phillip Morris vows to appeal $51.5-million verdict in favor of terminally ill California woman," Court TV Online Business, http://www.courttv.com/archive/business/tobacco/1999/021199_morris_ctv.html.

2 Richard L. Cupp, Jr., "A Morality Play's Third Act: Revisiting Addiction, Fraud and Consumer Choice in 'Third Wave' Tobacco Litigation," 46 *University of Kansas Law Review* 465 (1998).

3 *Cipollone v. Liggett Group*, 505 U.S. 504, 509–510 (1992).

4 *Ibid.*, 524–525.

5 *Ibid.*, 526.

6 George J. Annas, "Tobacco Litigation as Cancer Prevention: Dealing with the Devil," *Smoking Who Has the Right?*, eds. Jeffrey A. Schaler and Magda E. Schaler, 164 (Amherst, NY: Prometheus Books, 1998).

7 *Castano v. American Tobacco Co.*, 84 F. 3d 734, 752 (5th Cir., 1996)

8 *Burton v. R.J. Reynolds Tobacco Company*, 205 F.Supp. 2d 1253, 1255 (D. Kan. 2002).

9 David Hechler, "Billions and Billions: Tobacco Takes It on the Chin," *National Law Journal*, February 3, 2003.

10 Howard M. Erichson, "The End of the Defendant Advantage," *Tobacco Litigation*, 26 *William & Mary Environmental Law & Policy Review* 123, 133–134 (2001).

11 *U.S. v. Philip Morris U.S.A.*, 449 F.Supp. 2d 1 (D.D.C. 2006).

5 *Gibbs v. Republic Tobacco, L.P.*, 119 F.Supp.2d 1288 (M.D. Fla. 2000).

6 *Roysdon v. R.J. Reynolds Tobacco Company*, 849 F.2d 230, 236 (6th Cir. 1988).

7 *Toole v. Brown & Williamson*, 980 F.Supp. 419 (N.D. Ala. 1997).

8 *Tompkins v. R.J. Reynolds Tobacco Company*, 92 F.Supp.2d 70, 89 (2000).

9 *Wajda v. R.J. Reynolds Tobacco Company*, 103 F.Supp.2d 29 (D. Mass. 2000).

10 *State Farm Mutual Auto Ins. Co. v. Campbell*, 123 S.Ct. 1513 (2003).

11 *Ibid.*, 1524.

12 Available online at http://www.supreme courtus.gov/docket/02–1553.htm.

13 *Philip Morris U.S.A. v. Williams,—* U.S.—, 127 S.Ct. 1057 (2007).

14 Walter Williams, "Trashing the Rule of Law," *Capitalism Magazine*, October 7, 2003, http://capmag.com/article. asp?ID=3155.

15 John Alan Cohan. "Obesity, Public Policy, and Tort Claims," 12 Widener L.J. 103, 122 (2003).

Point: Advertising Restrictions Against Tobacco Products Help Protect Children and Are Constitutional

1 *Ohralik v. Ohio State Bar Ass'n*, 436 U.S. 447, 456 (1978).

2 *Ibid.*, 455–456.

3 *Virginia State Pharmacy Board v. Virginia Citizens Consumer Council*, 425 U.S. at 772, n. 24.

4 *Central Hudson Gas & Elec. Corp. v. Public Serv. Comm'n of N.Y.*, 447 U.S. 557 (1980).

5 *Capital Broadcasting Company v. Mitchell*, 333 F.Supp. 582 (D.D.C. 1971).

6 Steve Allen and Bill Adler, *The Passionate Nonsmoker's Bill of Rights* (New York: William Morrow and Company, 1989), 29.

7 Yabo Lin, "Put a Rein on That Unruly Horse: Balancing the Freedom of Commercial Speech and the Protection of Children in Restricting Cigarette Billboard Advertising," 52 Wash. U.J. & Contemp. L. 307, 350 (1997).

8 *Clay v. American Tobacco Company*, 188 F.R.D. 483 (S.D. Ill. 1999).

Counterpoint: Suits Against Big Tobacco Ignore Personal Responsibility and Unfairly Demonize a Legal Activity

1 Jeffrey A. Schaler, "Smoking Right and Responsibility," *Smoking Who Has the Right?*, eds. Jeffrey A. Schaler and Magda E. Schaler, 332 (Amherst, NY: Prometheus Books, 1993).

2 Quoted in Stephanie Gaskell, "Smoking Cops Hit Bars with 524 Tickets," *New York Post*, Sept. 17, 2003, O12.

3 Joseph L. Bast, "Smoking Under Siege: Why It Matters To You," Heartland Institute, September/October 1997, http://www.heartland.org/Article. cfm?artId=876.

4 Jeffrey A. Schaler, "Smoking Right and Responsibility," *Smoking Who Has the Right?*, eds. Jeffrey A. Schaler and Magda E. Schaler, 333 (Amherst, NY: Prometheus Books, 1993).

9 Edward M. Kennedy, "The Need for FDA Regulation of Tobacco Products," 3 *Yale Journal of Health Policy, Law & Ethics* 101, 103 (2002).

10 Charles King III and Michael Siegel, *The Master Settlement Agreement with the Tobacco Industry and Cigarette Advertising in Magazines*, http://content.nejm.org/cgi/content/full/345/7/504.

11 American Heart Association, "Tobacco Industry's Targeting of Youth, Minorities and Women," http://www.americanheart.org/presenter.jhtml?identifier=11226.

12 Surgeon General's Report on Reducing Tobacco Use, "Tobacco Advertising and Promotion Fact Sheet," http://www.cdc.gov/tobacco/data_statistics/sgr/sgr_2000/sgr_tobacco_chap.htm.

13 Vernellia R. Randall, "Smoking, the African-American Community, and the Proposed National Tobacco Settlement," 29 U. Tol. L. Rev. 677 (1998).

14 *Ibid.*, 682.

15 S. 2005—Section 2—Findings (15).

Counterpoint: Tobacco Advertising Is a Form of Protected Speech

1 425 U.S. 748 (1976).

2 *Capital Broadcasting Company v. Mitchell*, 333 F.Supp. 582, 587 (J. Wright, dissenting).

3 *Ibid.*, 590.

4 *Rubin v. Coors Brewing Company*, 514 U.S. 476 (1995).

5 *44 Liquormart, Inc. v. Rhode Island*, 517 U.S. 484 (1996).

6 *Ibid.*, 522 (J. Thomas, concurring).

7 *Lorillard Tobacco Co. v. Reilly*, 533 U.S. 525 (2001).

8 *Ibid.*

9 15 U.S.C. 1334(b).

10 *Lorillard Tobacco Co. v. Reilly.*

11 *Ibid.*

12 *Ibid.*, 564.

13 *Ibid.*, 566.

14 David S. Modzeleski, "Lorillard Tobacco v. Reilly: Are We Protecting the Integrity of the First Amendment and the Commercial Free Speech Doctrine at the Risk of Harming Our Youth?" 51 Cath. U.L. Rev. 987, 1020–1021 (2002).

15 Michael Hoefges, "Protecting Tobacco Advertising Under the Commercial Speech Doctrine: The Constitutional Impact of *Lorillard Tobacco Co.*," 8 Comm. L. & Pol'y 267, 305 (2003).

16 445 F.Supp.2d 1252, 1258 (W.D. Wash. 2006).

17 David L. Hudson, Jr., "Tobacco Ads," First Amendment Center Online, http://www.firstamendmentcenter.org/Speech/advertisingltopic.aspx?topic=tobacco_alcohol.

18 Margaret A. Little, "A Most Dangerous Indiscretion: The Legal, Economic, and Political Legacy of the Government's Tobacco Litigation," 33 Conn. L. Rev. 1143, 1144 (2001).

Conclusion: Smoking Bans in the Future

1 *Capital Broadcasting Co. v. Mitchell*, 333 F.Supp. at 587 (J. Wright, dissenting).

2 Family Prevention and Smoking Control Act of 2007, S. 625—Section 2 Findings.

3 Jessica Niezgoda, "Kicking Ash(Trays): Smoking Bans in Public Workplaces, Bars, and Restaurants: Current Laws, Constitutional Challenges, and Proposed Federal Regulation," 33 *Journal of Legislation* 99, 100–101 (2006).

RESOURCES ||||▷

Books and Articles

Allen, Steve, and Bill Adler, Jr. *The Passionate Nonsmoker's Bill of Rights.* New York: William Morrow and Company, 1989.

Cohan, John Alan. "Obesity, Public Policy, and Tort Claims." 12 Widener L.J. 103 (2003).

Colb, Sherry L. "Smoking Bans in New York: Outrageous or Reasonable?" Findlaw.com, April 9, 2003. Available online. URL: http://writ.news. findlaw.com/scripts/printer_friendly.pl?page=/colb/20030409.html. Accessed January 25, 2008.

Cupp, Richard L., Jr. "A Morality Play's Third Act: Revisiting Addiction Fraud and Consumer Choice in 'Third Wave' Tobacco Litigation." 46 U. Kan. L. Rev. 465 (1998).

Erichson, Howard. "The End of the Defendant Advantage in Tobacco Litigation." *William & Mary Environmental Law and Policy Review* 26, no. 123 (2001).

Ezra, David B. "'Get Your Ashes Out of My Living Room!' Controlling Tobacco Smoke In Multi-Unit Residential Housing." 54 *Rutgers Law Review* 135, 139 (2001).

Hechler, David. "Billions and Billions: Tobacco Takes It on the Chin." *National Law Journal*, February 3, 2003.

Henson, Rosemarie, et al. "Clean Indoor Air: Where, Why and How." 30 J.L. Med. & Ethics 75, 77 (2002).

Hilts, Philip J. *SmokeScreen: The Truth Behind the Tobacco Industry Coverup.* Reading, Mass.: Addison-Wesley Publishing Company, 1996.

Hoefges, Michael. "Protecting Tobacco Advertising Under the Commercial Speech Doctrine: The Constitutional Impact of *Lorillard Tobacco Co.*" 8 Comm. L. & Pol'y 267 (2003).

Kennedy, Edward. "The Need for FDA Regulation of Tobacco Products." 3 *Yale Journal of Health Policy, Law, & Ethics* 101 (2002).

Kluger, Richard. *Ashes to Ashes.* New York: Alfred A. Knopf, 1996.

Lin, Yabo. "Put a Rein on that Unruly Horse: Balancing The Freedom of Commercial Speech and the Protection of Children in Restricting Cigarette Billboard Advertising." 52 Wash. U.J. Urb. & Contemp. L. 307 (1997).

Little, Margaret. "A Most Dangerous Indiscretion: The Legal, Economic, and Political Legacy of the Government's Tobacco Litigation." 33 Conn. L. Rev. 1143 (2001).

Luka, Lori Ann. "The Tobacco Industry and the First Amendment: An Analysis of the 1998 Master Settlement Agreement." 14 Clev. St. U. J.L. & Health 297.

Modzeleski, David S. "Lorillard Tobacco v. Reilly: Are We Protecting the Integrity of the First Amendment and the Commercial Speech Doctrine at the Risk of Harming Our Youth?" 51 Cath. U.L. Rev. 987 (2002).

Niezgoda, Jessica. "Kicking Ash(Trays): Smoking Bans in Public Workplaces, Bars, and Restaurants: Current Laws, Constitutional Challenges, and Proposed Federal Regulation." 33 Journal of Legislation 99 (2006).

Randall, Vernellia R. "Smoking, the African-American Community, and the Proposed National Tobacco Settlement." 29 U. Tot. L. Rev. 677 (1998).

Redish, Martin. "First Amendment Theory and the Demise of the Commercial Speech Distinction: The Case of the Smoking Controversy." 24 N. Ky. L. Rev. 553 (1997).

Schaler, Jeffrey A., and Magda E. Schaler, eds. *Smoking: Who Has the Right?* Amherst, N.Y.: Prometheus Books, 1998.

Schwartz, Allison D. "Environmental Tobacco Smoke and Its Effect on Children: Controlling Smoke in the Home." 20 B.C. Envtl. Aff. L. Rev. 135 (1993).

Shoop, Julie Gannon. "1999 Brings Up and Downs for Tobacco Plaintiffs." *Trial*, April 1999.

Tondo, Carrie-Anne. "When Parents Are On a Level Playing Field, Courts Cry Foul at Smoking." 40 *Family Court Review* 238, 246 (2002).

Williamson, Matt. "When One Person's Habit Becomes Everyone's Problem: The Battle Over Smoking Bans in Bars and Restaurants." 14 *Villanova Sports & Entertainment Law Journal* 161 (2007).

Winokur, Samuel J. "Seeing Through the Smoke: The Need For National Legislation Banning Smoking in Bars and Restaurants." 75 *George Washington Law Review* 662 (2007).

RESOURCES ⫻⫻⫻▷

Web Sites

Americans for Nonsmokers' Rights
http://www.no-smoke.org
> This antismoking group provides good general information on issues relating to the smoking controversy.

Campaign for Tobacco-Free Kids
http://www.tobaccofreekids.org
> This antismoking site contains important information about smoking issues, especially ones that relate to young people.

Centers for Disease Control and Prevention on Smoking and Tobacco Use
http://www.cdc.gov/health/tobacco.htm
> This site contains information about the harmful health effects of tobacco.

Master Settlement Agreement
http://www.tobacco.neu.edu/tobacco_control/resources/msa/multistate_settlement.htm
> This link provides the full text of the Master Settlement Agreement.

R.J. Reynolds Tobacco Company
http://www.rjrt.com/legal/litOverview.asp
> The tobacco giant's official Web site has information on smoking litigation, cases, and underlying issues.

Tobacco Products Liability Project
http://www.tobacco.neu.edu
> This Web site contains a wealth of information regarding tort cases filed against tobacco companies. It provides analysis of each case, with commentary from lawyers working with the groups. This site is highly recommended for anyone wishing to track tobacco litigation.

Tobaccodocuments.org
http://www.tobaccodocuments.org
> This site features a searchable database of tobacco company documents made public as part of the Master Settlement Agreement.

Tobaccofree.org
http://www.tobaccofree.org
> This site encourages people to quit smoking and gives information on how to stop.

PAGE

13: AP Images/Elliott Minor
26: AP Images/Santilli
43: AP Images
66: AP Images/Jake O'Connell
79: AP Images/David Karp
99: AP Images/Pat Wellenbach

INDEX

DAVID L. HUDSON JR. is an author-attorney who has published widely on First Amendment and other constitutional law issues. Hudson is a research attorney with the First Amendment Center at Vanderbilt University and a First Amendment contributing editor to the American Bar Association's *Preview of the United States Supreme Court Cases.* He obtained his undergraduate degree from Duke University and his law degree from Vanderbilt University Law School.

ALAN MARZILLI, M.A., J.D., lives in Washington, D.C., and is a program associate with Advocates for Human Potential, Inc., a research and consulting firm based in Sudbury, Mass., and Albany, N.Y. He primarily works on developing training and educational materials for agencies of the federal government on topics such as housing, mental health policy, employment, and transportation. He has spoken on mental health issues in 30 states, the District of Columbia, and Puerto Rico; his work has included training mental health administrators, nonprofit management and staff, and people with mental illnesses and their families on a wide variety of topics, including effective advocacy, community-based mental health services, and housing. He has written several handbooks and training curricula that are used nationally and as far away as the territory of Guam. He managed statewide and national mental health advocacy programs and worked for several public interest lobbying organizations while studying law at Georgetown University. He has written more than a dozen books, including numerous titles in the *Point/Counterpoint* series.